Why Call Friday Good?

Why Call Friday Good?

Spiritual Reflections for Lent and Holy Week

CHUCK QUEEN

RESOURCE *Publications* • Eugene, Oregon

WHY CALL FRIDAY GOOD?
Spiritual Reflections for Lent and Holy Week

Resource Publications
An Imprint of Wipf and Stock Publishers
199 W. 8th Ave., Suite 3
Eugene, OR 97401

www.wipfandstock.com

ISBN 13: 978-1-61097-898-9

Manufactured in the U.S.A.

To Bennie League, a good friend,
who reads everything I write,
helping me become a better writer.
His compliments are much better than I deserve,
and his critique is always gracious.

And to the members of Immanuel Baptist Church,
Frankfort, Kentucky,
hearing these thoughts first as sermons,
inspired their present form as written reflections.

Contents

Introductory Note

THESE WRITTEN reflections on the words of Jesus from the cross began as sermons preached during Lent. The Easter reflection (chapter 8) was also a sermon, preached the same year. Sermons, of course, are oral communications, therefore considerable editing and some rewriting were necessary to offer them in their present form. Each reflection concludes with a prayer, followed by quotes from spiritual and theological writers I have found helpful. Anyone desiring to pursue the themes expounded in the reflections will find rich material in these writers.

It is my hope that individual Christians, as well as Bible study and discussion groups will find in these pages a valuable resource for their spiritual growth.

1

Feeling Forsaken

When it was noon, darkness came over the whole land until three in the afternoon. At three o'clock Jesus cried with a loud voice, "Eloi, Eloi, lema sabachthani?" which means, "My God, my God, why have you forsaken me?" When some of the bystanders heard it, they said, "Listen, he is calling for Elijah." And some ran, filled a sponge with sour wine, put it on a stick, and gave it to him to drink, saying, "Wait, let us see whether Elijah will come to take him down." Then Jesus gave a loud cry and breathed his last. And the curtain of the temple was torn in two, from top to bottom. Now when the centurion, who stood facing him, saw that in this way he breathed his last, he said, "Truly this man was God's Son!"
Mark 15:33–39[1]

WHEN MOTHER Teresa's private journals were published after her death, the startling revelation to so many was that her writings spoke of long periods where the

1. Unless otherwise indicated, all Scripture quotations are from the NRSV.

absence of God was more real to her than God's presence. In these extended dry periods, she did not sense nor feel God's presence.

The only word that Mark's Gospel tells us Jesus uttered from the cross was this word of abandonment: "My God, my God, why have you forsaken me?" It's a question, not a declaration and it reflects the sense of God's absence that overtook Jesus when he was hanging on the cross. What prompted this?

A missionary family was home on furlough, staying at the lake house of a friend. One day, Dad was puttering in the boathouse, Mom in the kitchen, and the three children, ages four, seven, and twelve, were on the lawn. Four-year-old Billy escaped his oldest sister's watchful eye and wandered down to the wooden dock. The shiny aluminum boat caught his eye, but unsteady feet landed him in eight-foot-deep water.

When the twelve-year-old screamed, Dad came running. Realizing what happened, he dove into the murky depths. Frantically he felt for his son, but twice had to return to the surface. Filling his lungs once more, he dove down and found Billy clinging to a wooden pier several feet under the water. Prying the boy's fingers loose, he bolted to the surface with Billy in his arms.

Safely ashore, his father asked, "Billy, what were you doing down there?" The little one replied, "Just waitin' on you, Dad, just waitin' on you."[2]

Could that be what provoked Jesus' sense of abandonment? Was he waiting on his Father to act, to come to his

2. Manning, *Ruthless Trust*, 95–96.

rescue, to bring deliverance? That seems to be the context of
the Psalmist who first uttered these words:

> My God, my God, why have you forsaken me?
> Why are you so far from helping me, from the
> words of my groaning? O my God, I cry by day,
> but you do not answer; and by night, but find no
> rest. Yet you are holy, enthroned on the praises of
> Israel. In you our ancestors trusted; they trusted,
> and you delivered them. To you they cried, and
> were saved; in you they trusted, and were not put
> to shame. Psalms 22:1–5

The Psalmist is crying out to God, but God is silent; looking
to God for deliverance, but God does not act.

But that was not what Jesus was expecting. Jesus
had already conceded to his fate. He wrestled with this in
Gethsemane. Mark tells us that he was "distressed and agi-
tated" and said to Peter, James, and John, whom he asked
to accompany him and pray for him, "I am deeply grieved,
even to death" (Mark 14:33–34). He asked his "Abba," his
good and compassionate Father/Mother, to take the cup
from him, but it was not to be.

The "cup" that Jesus refers to was not just the cup of
physical suffering unto death. It was that, but it was much
more. This is where Mel Gibson's version of the passion
got it wrong. Was it the humiliation, rejection, the scorn-
ing, mocking, the malicious hate and evil hurled upon him
by the powers that be? Was it the desertion of his closest
friends and partners? Surely all of these sufferings were part
of it, but there was still more.

In treating Jesus as a scapegoat, the actors in the crucifixion were not only despising and disparaging the love of

God that Jesus personified and embodied, they were denigrating and demeaning their own humanity. I believe that, for Jesus, to witness the depths of human corruption, the complete denunciation of the good, was even more painful than the physical sufferings or the humiliation and rejection he experienced.

Whereas Jesus represented humanity at its best, what was done to Jesus at Golgotha represented humanity at its worst. Jesus had come to show humanity the way of humility and love, but what he felt was the full force of humanity's arrogance and hate, and it was overwhelming.

The darkness that Mark says came over the land may well function in the narrative as a symbol for the evil unleashed upon Jesus. The darkness was so thick, the hate and evil so heavy and dense, that the light of God's presence could not break through into the consciousness of Jesus. Jesus, whom the Gospels present as continuously Spirit-filled, immersed in the reality of God's goodness and grace, cannot, on the cross, lay hold of God's presence.

The demonic spirit that possessed the actors in the crucifixion also dwells in us both individually and corporately. And at any unguarded moment it can erupt from the depths and take control. Who were the ones that ran the concentration camps of Nazi Germany, kept the gas ovens fed, made shades out of tattooed human skin, conducted ghastly experiments on living humans, and performed mass murders and executions? People just like you and me. Germany was the most educated and Christian of any nation on earth when the demons were set loose. With the right pressure and manipulation, how easy it is for any of us to become complicit in evil, to believe a lie, to turn our heads and pretend not to see. Jesus faced the worst that is in us and it broke his heart. Even the presence of God seemed to depart.

But was Jesus actually forsaken? Did God really depart? Was this in reality the eclipse of God? It felt like it to Jesus. Elie Wiesel, a surviver of Auschwitz, tells about the time the SS hung two Jewish men and a boy before the assembled inhabitants of the camp. The men died quickly, but the boy lasted half-an-hour. A man behind him asked, "Where is God? Where is he?" As the boy lingered in agony on the rope, the man cried again, "Where is God now?" Elie Wiesel says that a voice within him answered, "Here he is—he is hanging here on this gallows . . ."[3] This is the great paradox and mystery of the crucifixion reflected in Mark's version of the story. It was in God's absence that God was present.

In subtle ways throughout the story Mark tells us that Jesus is God's agent of redemption. When Jesus is brought before the high priest, where "all the chief priests, the elders, and the scribes were assembled" (14:53), Jesus is asked, "Are you the Messiah, the Son of the Blessed One?" (14:61). Without realizing it the high priest speaks truth which Jesus confirms (14:62). When Pilate, representative of imperial power, asks Jesus whether he is the King of the Jews, Jesus answers, "You say so" (15:2). Pilate continually refers to Jesus as "King of the Jews," but of course, he does not believe it. The soldiers mock Jesus as "King," dressing him in the color of royalty and placing a crown of thorns on his head (15:16–18). The inscription on the cross reads, "The King of the Jews" (15:26). Passersby, along with the

3. Referenced by Soelle, "On This Gallows," 175–76.

chief priests and scribes, mock him as "Messiah" and "King of Israel" as he hangs on the cross.

The great irony is that they are all proclaiming the gospel, but nobody believes it, because Jesus is being crucified. As Paul says in his first letter to the Corinthians, the Messiah crucified is scandalous, an offense to Jews and foolishness to Gentiles (1 Cor 1:23).

Then we come to the final confession by the Roman centurion, the executioner. Mark says, "Now when the centurion, who stood facing him, saw that in this way he breathed his last, he said, 'Truly, this man was God's Son'" (15:39).

Here is the irony, the mystery, and the paradox. God was indeed present. God was acting in Jesus to redeem. Paul expresses it this way in his second letter to the Corinthians: "In Christ God was reconciling the world to himself" (2 Cor 5:19). *Though Jesus is passive, bearing it all, God is active, reaching out to the world in and through Jesus' death. God is active in the passivity of Jesus.*

I believe that what Jesus experienced, God experienced. I do not believe in a distant, removed Almighty—an "Unmoved Mover." I believe in a God who is deeply moved and engaged in the life of the creation.

Rob Bell, the evangelical mega-church pastor of Mars Hill Bible Church in Michigan, made a big splash in the evangelical Christian world with his book, *Love Wins: A Book About Heaven, Hell, and the Fate of Every Person Who Ever Lived*. The marketing of the book was ingenious. Bell's short video promo caught the attention of many and set off a hailstorm of Twitter and blog posts. For the first few weeks of the book's release Bell did numerous media and television interviews. One such interview was conducted by Martin Bashir of MSNBC.

Before Bashir asked him about his book, he asked him to respond to the quake disaster in Japan. He put it this way, "Which do you believe: That God is all powerful, but doesn't care about the people in Japan and their suffering, or that God cares about their suffering, but is not all powerful?" That's how Bashir framed the question, as if these were the only two options. Rob Bell responded by saying that he begins with the belief that when we shed a tear God sheds a tear, that God is a Divine Being who is profoundly empathetic, compassionate, and stands in solidarity with us. That didn't fit into Bashir's narrow, little box so he kept pressing him. Finally Bell said, "It is a paradox at the heart of the Divine and it's best left at that."

It was a terribly conducted interview that revealed more about Martin Bashir than it did about Rob Bell. Bashir framed the questions in a way that required yes/no, either/ or responses. The questions, however, dealt with truth that defied such simplistic answers. Bashir's approach, I think, is quite typical of people who have no experience or understanding of authentic spiritual reality. Genuine spiritual truth and experience are much more complex, filled with paradox, ambiguity, and mystery. (Jesus, by the way, never offered simplistic answers. He spoke in stories, short witty aphorisms, and shocking hyperbolic sayings filled with paradox, irony, and mystery.) Healthy Christianity (or healthy religion, for that matter) does not need or invite simple, trite, all-encompassing answers to the universal questions of human suffering.

Christianity does not have easy answers, but it does have the cross, where God in Christ enters into the tragedy of the human condition and bears it, endures it, owns it, and absorbs it.

In his novel *Jayber Crow*, Wendell Berry observes that Christ did not descend from the cross except into the grave (that is, he didn't overcome his killers by miraculous power). If he had, says Berry, he would be the absolute tyrant of the world and we his slaves. For if he had, then "even those who hated him and hated one another and hated their own souls would have to believe in him then. From that moment," writes Berry, "the possibility that we might be bound to him and he to us and us to one another by love forever would be ended."[4]

Berry argues that God is present "only in the ordinary miracle of the existence of God's creatures," in "the poor, the hungry, the hurt, the wordless creatures" and in this "groaning and travailing beautiful world." Berry cuts against the grain of our privatized, compartmentalized way of seeing life, reflecting a more universal and inclusive worldview. Berry writes, "We are all involved in all and any good, and in all and any evil. For any sin, we all suffer. That is why our suffering is endless. It is why God grieves and Christ's wounds still are bleeding"[5]

God participates with us in our suffering. God is not "out there," but in us and with us, sharing in our pain and loss. In Jesus' once-upon-a-cross humiliation and in the ever present bleeding wounds of the living Christ we find a brother. In his cries of forsakenness we discover a comrade and friend.

4. Berry, *Jayber Crow*, 295.
5. Ibid., 295.

He descended into our "hell" and suffered it, in order to empty it of its malevolent power. Our disappointments and discouragements, our failures and defeats, our feelings of abandonment and rejection, do not separate us from Christ, but draw us into fellowship with him. Theologian Jurgen Moltmann says, "Good Friday is the most comprehensive and most profound expression of Christ's fellowship with every human being."[6] He stands in union and solidarity with every suffering soul.

Though Jesus felt forsaken on the cross, he did not forsake God. Popular spiritual writer Brennan Manning says that the most brilliant student he ever taught in Seminary was a young man named Augustus Gordan. When Manning told this story, Gordan lived as a hermit six months each year in a solitary cabin, deep in the Smoky Mountains. The remaining half-year he traveled the country preaching the gospel on behalf of Food for the Poor, a missionary outreach feeding the hungry and homeless in Haiti, Jamaica, and other Caribbean islands. On a visit, Manning asked him if he could define the Christian life in a single sentence. He defined it in a single word: trust.[7]

This is what Jesus is doing on the cross, even while feeling forsaken. He still clings to God. "My God, my God" is a cry of trust. It is an affirmation of his persistence that the God of justice and peace, of judgment and grace, whose dream is of a redeemed, restored, reconciled world—this God, is his God.

Manning says, "If the night is bad and our nerves are shattered and darkness comes and pain is all around and

6. Moltmann, "Prisoner of Hope," 151.

7. Manning, *Ruthless Trust*, 4.

the Holy One is conspicuous by his absence and we want to know the true feelings of the inscrutable God toward us, we must turn and look at Jesus."[8] And *if we want to overcome, then we must do what Jesus did: keep trusting.*

Some words from Isaiah are appropriate here (if we take our cue from the writers of the New Testament, then we are safe to apply this to the living Christ),

> He gives power to the faint, and strengthens the powerless. Even youths will faint and be weary, and the young will fall exhausted; but those who wait for the Lord shall renew their strength, they shall mount up with wings like eagles, they shall run and not be weary, they shall walk and not faint. Isa 40:29–31.

Sometimes we soar, sometimes we run, sometimes we walk, and then there are times when all we can do is hold our ground and cry, "My God, my God." And that is enough.

Our Good God, in our times of crisis, when the darkness descends upon us and we can't see our way forward, when you seem so distant and far, when we feel forsaken, help us find in Jesus the embodiment of your love and your participation in and experience of our suffering. Give us the courage, hope, and faith to cling to you and your grace, even when we can't see any sign, or hear any voice, or feel any sense of your presence. Give us the will and grace to trust, like Jesus. Amen

The Father forsakes the Son 'for us'–that is, he allows him to die so that he may become the God and Father of the forsaken. The Father 'gives up' the Son that through him

---

8. Ibid., 91.

he may become the Father of all those who are 'given up' (Rom. 1.18ff). This transforms 'the almighty Father' too; for Christ was 'crucified in the weakness of God' (II Cor. 13.4). The Son is surrendered to this death in order to become brother and saviour of all the men and women who are condemned and accursed. . . . On the cross the Father and Son are so widely separated that the direct relationship between them breaks off. Jesus died a 'Godless death.' And yet on the cross the Father and the Son are so much at one that they present a single surrendering movement.[9]

The definition 'God is love' acquires its full weight only if we continually make ourselves aware of the path that leads to that definition: Jesus' forsakenness on the cross, the surrender of the Son, and the love of the Father, which does everything, gives everything and suffers everything for lost men and women. God is love: that means God is self-giving. It means God exists for us: on the cross.[10]

By virtue of this mutual indwelling (perichoresis) of the Father and the Son, Jesus' sufferings are divine sufferings, and God's love is love that is able to suffer and is prepared to suffer. The power of the divine Spirit in Jesus is transformed from an active power that works wonders to a suffering power that endures wounds.[11]

9. Moltmann, *The Way of Jesus Christ*, 173–74.

10. Ibid., 175.

11. Ibid., 177.

2

Preemptive Forgiveness

> When they came to the place that is called The Skull, they crucified Jesus there with the criminals, one on his right and one on his left. Then Jesus said, Father forgive them; for they do not know what they are doing. And they cast lots to divide his clothing. Luke 23:33–34

I N THE movie, *Unforgiven*, Clint Eastwood plays William Munny, a man known to be notoriously vicious before he married and settled down. His wife helped him change. Since her death from smallpox, he has devoted himself to working a farm in the Kansas countryside and to caring for his two small children.

One day a young man shows up calling himself "The Schofield Kid." He had been told that Munny was "cold as the snow, with no weak nerve, no fear." The Kid wants Munny to join him as a partner in claiming a bounty of one thousand dollars offered by some prostitutes to anyone who would come to Big Whiskey, Wyoming, and bring vengeance on two cowboys that attacked, cut, and severely scarred one of them on the face. At first Munny tells the Kid,

"I ain't like that anymore." Then he changes his mind. He pulls out his guns and practices shooting. Unaware of their father's past, his young daughter wonders to her brother, "Did pa used to kill folks?" So he leaves his children and on the way picks up Ned, an old friend, his former partner in killing, and the two of them catch up with the Kid.

The two cowboys they aim to kill work for "Little Bill," a gun slinger who is the law and order in Big Whiskey. After a shootout with Little Bill's men, when one of the cowboys is killed, Ned decides to go home, leaving Munny and the Kid to finish the job. Ned is captured by Little Bill and in Little Bill's attempt to find out who killed his men, he whips Ned to death and exposes his bloody body upright in an open casket in front of the saloon. When the prostitute who brings Munny his bounty informs him of the death of his friend, Munny decides to go after Little Bill.

In preparation, Munny chugs down a bottle of whiskey, throwing away the empty bottle as he enters town. He walks into the crowded saloon where Little Bill is congratulating the posse on its performance. Munny kills the saloon owner for decorating the saloon with Ned. Little Bill says to Munny, "You're William Munny, from out of Missouri, killed women and children." Munny says, "That's right. I killed women and children. I've killed just about everything that walked or crawled at one time or another. And I'm here to kill you, Little Bill, for what you did to Ned."

In the shootout that ensues, Munny kills five men and wounds Little Bill. The rest run out the back. As Munny stares over Little Bill, Little Bill says, "I don't deserve this. To die like this. I was building a house." Munny responds, "'Deserve' got nothing to do with this." Little Bill says, "I'll see you in hell, William Munny." Munny says, "Yeah," and then kills Little Bill. The film ends with Munny riding out in the rain, yelling out to the town's people hiding in the shadows that they better give his friend Ned a proper burial or he'll come back and kill them all.

The film evokes the question: Can the spiral of violence that plagues our planet, that fractures and severs relationships, ravaging families, communities, and whole societies, ever be neutralized and overcome? Are we caught in a web from which we cannot tear loose?

Consider our own nation's commitment to violence, formerly in Iraq and now in Afghanistan. According to the Pentagon's November, 2010 progress report, violent incidents in Afghanistan have increased seventy percent in the last year. David Cortright, the director of policy studies at Notre Dame's Kroc Institute for International Peace Studies states that nearly every independent study of the war concurs that the presence of American and other foreign troops there is a major cause of the insurgency. The number of Taliban fighters has increased in proportion to the expansion of our military forces, and the stronger we push the more influence the Taliban gains in the region. NATO commander Gen. David Petraeus says that we are up against a growing "industrial-strength insurgency," now numbering more than thirty thousand fighters.

The human toll of the violence has been immense. Based on official reports, in 2010 more than ten thousand people died as a result of the violence. As in every war, innocent civilians bear the brunt of the violence. According to the U.N. Assistant Mission in Afghanistan there were 2,412 Afghan civilians killed over the first ten months of

2010. The U.N. High Commissioner for Refugees states there are now at least 319,000 internally displaced persons in Afghanistan, of whom 120,000 fled their homes between June 2009 and September 2010.

In "just war" doctrine, the moral criterion of "last resort" is essential. It requires that all non-military options be exhausted before military force can be justified. From the beginning of the war in Afghanistan, military means have been the first resort, not the last. No one in power asked whether better options were available for countering the violent extremism of the Taliban and helping to stabilize Afghanistan. We have been committed to violence. Violence almost always provokes counter-violence—and there seems to be no end to the cycle.[1]

Into our violent, broken, and shattered world enters Jesus. The good news proclaimed here in Luke's Gospel is that God has acted for and in this violent planet in the life, death, and resurrection of Jesus to break the cycle of violence in which we all seem to be trapped.

In the Gospels, Jesus refuses to get sucked into the spiral of violence. He refuses to succumb to the power of darkness. On the night of his betrayal and arrest, one of his disciples draws his sword and strikes the slave of the high priest, cutting off his ear. Jesus exclaims, "No more of this!" And to make his point, he touches the man's ear and restores it. Violence never brings healing. Never. It may, on some occasions, bring an end to overt violence, but it often, as we have witnessed in Afghanistan, causes

1. The statistical information above was gleaned from two articles in Sojourners by Cortright, "Finding the Way Out" and Stoner, "The Human Toll."

the violence to escalate. It cannot heal or redeem. There is no redemptive violence.

Only forgiveness can exhaust the constantly spinning spiral of violence and offer redemptive possibilities. But we rarely do it, because it is so costly. Look at Jesus on the cross, bearing the violence, enduring the punishment and torture inflicted by the powers that be. What does he do in reaction? *He responds to the violence with a preemptive strike of forgiveness. The enormity of the sin against Jesus is countered only by the magnitude of Jesus' grace toward his killers.*

Forgiveness, of course, is not unique to Jesus, nor to the Judaism of which he was a part. In Judaism, forgiveness was open to anyone who returned to the way of the Lord. It was connected to the Temple and its sacrificial ritual in ways that we are not quite sure of (scholars debate the particulars), but it always included repentance and restitution for wrongs committed against other human beings.

With Jesus comes a radical shift in understanding and appropriating forgiveness. Jesus incarnates and expresses forgiveness directly, disconnecting it from the Temple cult. In the Synoptic Gospels, Jesus heals and forgives a paralytic who is brought to him by his friends. All three Gospels interpret the healing as a demonstration of the authority of the Son of Man to forgive sins. Matthew's version of the story, however, emphasizes that the authority to forgive does not belong to Jesus alone. Matthew concludes the story by saying that the crowds "glorified God, who had given such authority to human beings" (Matt 9:8), not just Jesus. Jesus, as the "Son of Man" acts as the representative of all human beings in forgiving the paralytic his sins. *The authority and freedom to forgive is granted to all of us; there is no need for a sacrificial ritual to mediate it.*

This marked a major change in the way most Jews believed how forgiveness worked. But perhaps the most radical change of all came through the way Jesus related forgiveness to repentance. There is no question that Jesus placed a great deal of emphasis on the necessity of repentance, but the remarkably fresh insight that comes with Jesus' practice of forgiveness on the cross is that forgiveness precedes repentance. Jesus proclaims and embodies the unconditional, forgiving nature of God. *Before repentance, before confession, before there is any acknowledgment of wrong doing, Jesus cries, "Father, forgive them."*

How scandalous and offensive this is to those who want everyone to get what they deserve. But this is no "cheap grace." Repentance is still necessary in effecting healing and reconciliation. Jesus forgave his tormentors, but we do not know who among them, if any, entered into that reality and personally experienced forgiveness. There can be no experience or personal appropriation of forgiveness without repentance; there can be no reconciliation without conversion. So there is a cost. *Forgiveness is not only costly to the one who gives it, bearing and absorbing the injustice; it is costly to the one who receives it, for repentance is necessary.*

There are two primary ways we avoid forgiveness. First, *we avoid forgiveness when we fail to face the wrong/s we have done, when we fail to admit to the one/s we have offended and to God the hurt and pain our actions have caused.* We do this in various ways. Perhaps we are too entrapped by our greed, pride, envy, jealousy, or our self-consumption. Or maybe we take pleasure in vengeance and retaliation, or in destroying the competition. We could be like Little Bill and be so sadistically twisted that we find some measure of satisfaction in controlling others and heaping pain upon them. For whatever reason, there are those of us who simply refuse to face and admit our guilt.

We avoid it, also, when we deny that we need it. Have you ever been forgiven, and then wondered what you were forgiven for? When it is pointed out to us, typically our first response is to offer some justification for our actions. In the movie *Unforgiven*, just after the Kid kills one of the two cowboys in the Bar-T's outhouse, the Kid and Munny flee to a mountainside and drink whiskey. Contrary to his earlier bravado, this was the first man the Kid ever killed. He had been mostly talk and now he is visibly shaken by his deed. He says to Munny, "It doesn't seem right. He'll never breathe again. . . . All on account of pulling a trigger." Munny responds, "It's a hell of a thing, killing a man." The Kid finally exclaims in justification, "I guess he had it coming." We seem to always be looking for ways to justify our evil deeds.

Then too, in keeping with our refusals, denials, and justifications, we may be willfully ignorant and really think we are in the right. This is the danger of unhealthy religion and power politics. Jesus said, "Father, forgive them, for they do not know what they are doing." The religious leaders thought they were ridding their community of a heretic, a false Messiah. Pilate thought he was ridding the Empire of a trouble-maker. Or if Pilot did not regard Jesus as a real threat, he surely was doing what he thought was necessary to appease his constituency and secure their cooperation for his agenda. The Roman soldiers were just doing their job, following orders, and having a little fun with someone whom they considered less than human—an enemy of the State who deserved to die. In one sense, they did not know what they were doing. But such ignorance or delusion doesn't make them, or us, less culpable.

So we avoid the cost of forgiveness by failing or refusing, for whatever reason, to admit, acknowledge, and repent of our wrongdoing. *Another way we avoid the cost of forgiveness is by wallowing in our guilt.* Maybe this was why Munny was lured back into his killing ways. He told himself he was doing it to get the money for his kids. He had changed to some degree; his wife had an impact on him, but there are hints throughout the story that he had never really experienced forgiveness. When the Kid says to Munny regarding the man he had just killed, "I guess he had it coming," Munny replies, "We all have it coming." The very title of the film, *Unforgiven*, suggests that Munny was drowning in his regret and could not live with his past.

Theologian L. Gregory Jones has observed that people can become so convicted by their complicity in evil and so paralyzed by their guilt that they end up "rebelling against their temporary obsession with guilt and return to their desire to destroy victims precisely for being victims."[2] In other words, a person can become so devastated by guilt and shame, that the despair of self-contempt propels the individual into reckless, destructive actions, either toward oneself or others, or both.

But if we can recognize the ways we avoid the hard work of forgiveness and learn to embrace the process (forgiveness is more of a journey than a single act), our lives

2. Jones, *Embodying Forgiveness*, 116.

and relationships can be healed and transformed. We see this possibility in Luke's story of the prostitute who is forgiven by Jesus. Simon, the Pharisee, looks upon her with contempt and condemnation, and questions Jesus for allowing her to anoint his feet with expensive perfume and wipe them with her hair. Jesus explains to Simon that her overwhelming, spontaneous expression of gratitude was the result of her experience of forgiveness. Jesus says that the one who is forgiven much, loves much (Luke 7:47).

The transforming experience of forgiveness is also reflected in the story of the Prodigal in Luke 15, who returns home after being in the far country. In desperation, he realizes that his Father's hired servants have it better than he does. So he turns toward home, prepared to confess his offense to his father and to ask to be treated as a hired servant in his house. It doesn't seem, however, that in his initial turning toward home (where he "comes to his senses") he faces the hurt and scandal his betrayal has caused his father; he seems more interested in being delivered from his own despair.

When the father sees his son coming home, he runs to him, embraces him, kisses him, showers him with love, restoring him to his place as a son in the household. He can do that, because he has already forgiven him. And in this overwhelming display of grace and restoration, the son appears to be deeply sorrowful and contrite. (In his second confession spoken directly to the father, he does not even mention the part about being a hired servant.)

Can the spiral of violence be halted in light of the power of darkness? Can the cycles of habitual violence and counter-violence be altered and redeemed in light of all the hostility, prejudice, cruelty, manipulation, and evil in the world? There are a few subtle hints in *Unforgiven* that suggest the possibility of redemption. After Ned attempts to kill one of the cowboys, but cannot, he decides to walk away. He apparently no longer has the will or capacity to kill. And after the Kid kills a man for the first time, he decides that he does not want to live as a killer. These are small signs, but they shed a ray of hope on the human condition.

At the end of Luke's Gospel, when God vindicates Jesus' commitment to nonviolence by raising him from the dead, the risen Christ appears to the disciples who had betrayed and deserted him in his greatest hour of need. Rather than rebuking them, he greets them, "Peace be with you" (Luke 24:36). He doesn't even bring up their betrayal. He eats with them, showing them that he has forgiven them. Then he challenges them with a new assignment. He charges them with the task of proclaiming repentance and the forgiveness of sins to all peoples (Luke 24:47–49). Not just to the Jews, but to everyone, for there are no boundaries.

The good news is this: Their desertion is countered by Jesus' inclusion. Their fear is met with a call to faith. Their rejection is supplanted by Jesus' acceptance. Their guilt is replaced by Jesus' forgiveness. Their faithlessness is superseded by Jesus' faithfulness to them. They abandoned Jesus, but he did not abandon them. Jesus in essence says, "Claim your forgiveness. We have work to do. You are to be witnesses of these things." Luke says that they worshiped him and returned to Jerusalem, the very place of their betrayal, with great joy.

The words of Jesus on the cross reveal to us that Jesus will not even abandon his killers and tormentors. The living

Christ is saying today, "Father, forgive them . . ." The question is: Can we accept such acceptance? The gift is given freely, unconditionally, but accepting the gift means that we accept the responsibility that goes with it. *In order to receive the forgiveness offered to us unconditionally, we must be willing to embody forgiveness. The experience of forgiveness requires the practice of forgiveness.*

Christ has come to set us free from the cycles of violence and counter-violence, from the habits of retaliation and revenge that diminish our lives and lay waste our world. The hope of our world and the future of our planet depend upon our acquiring the spiritual courage and inner strength to forgive one another as Christ has forgiven us.

Our Good God, though you created us for communion with you and one another, we do not typically give and receive freely with one another. So often we seek to secure our lives at the expense of others. We are the heirs of histories and habits of sin and evil that make it difficult to break out of cycles of rejection and condemnation that diminish and decimate life. We know that we were made for more, that we were created for a greater purpose and destiny, designed to love and be loved, to forgive and be forgiven. Give us the grace to know empathetically the hurt and sorrow of our brothers and sisters, and to repent of our complicity in evil and the diminution of life it has caused. Give us the capacity today to both hear and speak Jesus' words of forgiveness from the cross. Amen

The attempt to divide the world into tidy categories of oppressor and oppressed or victimizer and victim oversimplifies the more complex realities of histories and habits of sin and evil. While it is undeniably true that many people have suffered—and continue to suffer—immensely through exploitation and violence, systemic and otherwise—none of us is free from the trap of being both victimizer and victim.[3]

Just as there is no one way in which social and personal relations have become impoverished and continue to be impoverished (and also no one way in which people are victimizers and victims), so there is no one way of appropriating Christ's forgiveness by the power of the Spirit. Such appropriation invites us not to forget the past, but to remember it well so that we can envision and embody a future different from the past. In that sense, we need the Spirit both to return to us our memories and also to enliven our imaginations.[4]

The practice of forgiveness entails unlearning all those things that divide and destroy communion and learning to see and live as forgiven and forgiving people. The goal of this unlearning and learning is the holiness of communion—with God, with others, and with the whole Creation. We are called to do this most specifically, though by no means exclusively, among those who seek to live in truthful communion with God and with one another in Christian community.[5]

---

3. Jones, *Embodying Forgiveness*, 116.
4. Ibid., 149.
5. Ibid., 164.

3

The Gospel in a Snapshot

Two others also, who were criminals, were led away to be put to death with him. When they came to the place that is called The Skull, they crucified Jesus there with the criminals, one on his right and one on his left. . . .

One of the criminals who were hanged there kept deriding him and saying, "Are you not the Messiah? Save yourself and us!" But the other rebuked him, saying, "Do you not fear God, since you are under the same sentence of condemnation? And we indeed have been condemned justly, for we are getting what we deserve for our deeds, but this man has done nothing wrong." Then he said, "Jesus, remember me when you come into your kingdom." He replied, "Truly I tell you, today you will be with me in Paradise." Luke 23:32–43

In Luke's Gospel, Jesus makes three statements from the cross. The first we considered in the last chapter: "Father, forgive them, for they do not know what they are doing." The second, like the first, is also a word of grace that is uttered to a criminal hanging on the cross next to Jesus.

Only Luke has this promise of Jesus to the criminal. In fact, Mark and Matthew have a different account. In their version, both criminals mock and ridicule Jesus. Mark's Gospel reads, "Those who were crucified with him also taunted him" (Mark 15:32).

Is that a problem? Well, yes and no. It does pose a problem for the historian who wants to know what actually happened. But a Gospel is not primarily a historical document. It contains history, but a Gospel is primarily a proclamation of the meaning and significance, theologically and spiritually, of the Christ Event—the life, death, and resurrection of Jesus of Nazareth. The Gospel writers saw no problem in altering and embellishing the stories in order to proclaim the good news of Jesus, the Christ.

It's possible that this was one version of the story passed down to Luke. First century Palestine was primarily an oral culture, and before the Jesus stories were ever written down they were passed down by word of mouth. In the oral transmission of the stories, details were deleted, added, and changed. Sometimes the changes were unintentional, other times intentional, reflecting theological and spiritual concerns.

I am inclined to think that Luke himself may have fashioned the story this way to give the reader a miniature version, a snapshot of the good news. For Luke, as well as the other Gospel writers, proclaiming the gospel message was more important than preserving correct memories.

While the other criminal insults and mocks Jesus, this criminal exonerates Jesus: "We are getting what we deserve for our deeds, but this man has done nothing wrong." Three times in Luke's passion narrative Jesus is exonerated. First by Pilate, then by this criminal hanging with Jesus, and finally by the centurion at the end of the crucifixion scene who says, "Certainly this man was innocent" (23:47).[1] This is Luke's way of saying that Jesus was blameless. Jesus' blamelessness is set against the backdrop of the guilt of the criminals hanging with him. *In this manner Luke paints a summary portrait of the good news: Jesus dying among the wretched and the guilty, bearing the injustice without vengeance, retribution, or even anger in his heart.*

Jesus was committed to God's cause—to God's nonviolent reign of peace and justice, to the spiritual restoration of Israel, and ultimately the reconciliation of the world. He was willing to bear the wrath, animosity, and judgment of the powers that be in order to expose the powers of evil and break the cycles of hate and violence. Jesus was broken for the healing and mending of wounded, shattered lives and communities. He suffered for the salvation of the suffering world.

Jesus became a scapegoat to put an end to all scapegoating; he became a sacrifice to put an end to that whole system of sacrificing the innocent victim. Spiritually, socially, and psychologically, humans have always needed to find some way to deal with sin and guilt. Historically, humanity has employed sacrificial systems to that end. In ancient systems of religion, human sacrifices were offered to placate the deity (such as the firstborn, the virgin, the only child, etc., but never the adult man; these were mostly, if not all, patriarchal

1. In Mark and Matthew he says, "Truly this man was God's Son" (Mark 15:39; Matt 27:54).

cultures). In the evolution of religious consciousness, animals took the place of humans.

It doesn't seem that our spiritual consciousness has evolved a great deal over the last several millennia. The educationally advanced Germans made scapegoats of the Jews, and consider all the horrendous scapegoating that has taken place in the genocides of the past several decades.

The scapegoat mechanism was incorporated into Christianity when Christians adopted an interpretation of Jesus' death that made Jesus a victim of a stern, punitive Magistrate who required redemptive violence. This was primitive religion, more or less Christianized. This type of Christianity is by its very nature dualistic, leading to exclusion and often violence, because adherents think they have to destroy the evil element. Rarely do they see the evil in their own hearts; it is generally projected onto the other. This makes the God of Christians appear violent, vindictive, and petty.

What does Jesus do on the cross? According to Luke, he forgives. *He bears the wrath and the hostility of the worldly powers—without lashing out, without vengeance, without returning evil for evil, without projecting fear or hate or evil back onto his persecutors and killers.* Jesus exposed the folly and evil of scapegoat religion. As the quintessential "Son of Man," the archetype of authentic humanity, he publicly exposed the great illusion of evil disguised as "holiness" by the religious gatekeepers and as "securing the peace" by the imperial powers represented by Pilot and the Roman soldiers. Jesus unmasked the true nature of egotistical religious and political power much the way the civil rights marchers who

crossed the bridge in Selma, Alabama, unmasked the illusion of white supremacy.

Still today, we have deceptive versions of Christianity
that permit, even encourage, Christians to buy into the
illusion that might makes right. In such systems, control
and manipulative power are viewed as legitimate means to
an end. These versions of Christianity are primarily aimed
at spreading doctrinal beliefs and influencing others to
conform to their belief system, or else face God's wrath.
And too often, assuming themselves as the sole possessors
of the truth, they see no problem or contradiction in becoming the instruments of divine wrath on the others who
do not conform.

In such oppressive systems of Christianity (such as
the kind reflected in the "Left Behind" novels) Jesus' death
is nothing more than a legal transaction that supposedly
satisfies God's need for a sacrifice. In these belief systems,
God requires the violent sacrifice of his Son in order to
procure forgiveness. This is what evangelical philosopher
and theologian Dallas Willard calls a "sin management"
system that does nothing to effect real change in an individual or society.[2]

*If the life and teachings of Jesus tell us anything about
the nature of God, it is surely that God has no need for cosmic, judicial retribution. If God can forgive, then God can
forgive. There is no need for a divine payoff, or satisfaction of
divine honor, or appeasement of divine wrath.*

Sin has never been a problem for God. It has been the
problem for humanity, preventing us from reaching our
human potential, fueling greed, the lust for power, and the

2. See his discussion in Willard, *The Divine Conspiracy*, 35–59.

hoarding of wealth in an alienated and alienating ethos. *Jesus did not come to change the mind or heart of God about humanity, but to change the mind and heart of humanity about God, each other, and our world.*

Jesus' death was not demanded by God; it was the logical culmination of a life that challenged the arrogant, coercive, controlling powers with the power of a humble, inclusive, unconditional compassion. What must die is our egoism. We must die to our selfish ambitions, our need to be right and in control, and to all our projections of guilt, hate, and evil onto the other, whoever the other may be. *Jesus' death becomes the means of our redemption when we follow Jesus to the cross and die there with him; when we refuse to return evil for evil and bear, with Jesus, the evil and hate of the powers that be.* Jesus, through forgiveness and nonviolence, offers us a way through the darkness, a way to terminate the cycles of hate and violence, and bring healing and transformation to our personal lives, families, communities, societies, and our planet.

Jesus' death is not the solution to a problem residing in God; it's the solution to the problem of evil residing in us. It is the ultimate, prototypical symbol of the nature and reality of God. *Its redemptive power lies in its capacity to lure us into the mystery and miracle of unconditional forgiveness, reconciling grace, and healing love.*

The criminal says to Jesus, "Remember me." That little phrase is found in the Old Testament on the lips of Joseph, Hannah, Nehemiah, Job, and the Psalmist. It is a humble appeal for grace, for God to save, rescue, or deliver. Jesus responds with radical grace.

Not every one wants a gospel of radical grace, however. United Methodist Bishop Will Willimon tells about the time he took a course in Clinical Pastoral Education (CPE) when he was in seminary preparing for the ministry. His CPE was in a hospital setting. One day a man, forced by the staff to enter in a wheelchair, came cursing and shouting at the staff all the way in. He brought his secretary with him for important business that no one but he could do. Willimon was told not to visit him because he was a CEO who would be on the phone most of the day. Besides, he didn't care for clergy or want them around. He was deathly ill, but refused to accept the diagnosis and had a specialist fly in from Minnesota. Each day there was a stream of corporate underlings scampering in and out of his room receiving their assignments. Willimon tried to visit him once, but the big-shot executive cursed at him, screaming that the hospital had better get his problem fixed and that he had no time to waste on little would-be CPE preacher boys.

Willimon remembers the afternoon that he heard loud wailing coming from his room. A nurse ran down the hall calling, "Get me the chaplain, quick; Mr. Smith has finally got the truth and has had a breakdown." Willimon asked if he could help. She informed him that she needed a real chaplain.

So the older, wiser chaplain was called and went into Mr. Smith's room. Things got very quiet. Finally, the chaplain emerged and on his way back down the hall he grumbled to Willimon, "Well, God got another one." Apparently, he wasn't very happy about it.[3]

---

3. Willimon, *Thank God It's Friday*, 74–75.

I can understand why someone would grumble. *Radical grace means that there are no winners and losers.* You can't do anything to make God love you more or less. There is no first place or second place or third place, no pecking order or hierarchy of special people. So if you have worked all your life trying to be better than everyone else, it can be a real letdown. It means that life is not a competition for places and positions in the kingdom, like James and John had imagined when they asked Jesus for seats on his left and right. For some folks, that's hard to take. If you are aspiring for greatness, then radical grace is not what you covet. Radical grace levels the playing field; it gathers us all into the same boat. If you are accustomed to going first class that could be a problem.

Jesus says to the criminal: "Truly I tell you, today you will be with me *in Paradise.*" Maybe you heard about the florist who mixed up two orders on a busy day. One arrangement was supposed to go to a new business just opening up and the other to a funeral, but they were mixed up. The next day, the guy with the new business came rushing in very upset. He exclaimed, "What's the big idea? The flowers that arrived for our reception said, 'Rest in peace.'" The florist said, "Well, if you think that's bad, you should have seen the people at the funeral when they got the flowers that said, 'Good luck in your new location.'" Jesus tells the dying criminal that they are going to a new location. Paradise, he says.

This is the only mention of Paradise in the Gospels. The central message of Jesus in Luke (as well as Mark and Matthew) is the kingdom of God. The kingdom of God, as employed by Jesus in his preaching and teaching, is a rather dynamic image and fluid symbol, but it is rooted in the prophetic tradition of God's peaceable reign over Israel and the nations. The focus is on this world, not a heavenly other-world. And when Jesus elsewhere speaks of resurrection (Luke 20:27–40), he associates it with the age to come, the time of the realization/fulfillment of God's kingdom/ reign on earth.

Paul, in his correspondence with the Corinthians, talks about being caught up to "the third heaven," which he also calls "Paradise" (2 Cor 12:1–4). The Jews imagined different levels of heavenly reality. Paul tells them that he doesn't know if he was in the body or out of the body. I suspect he had some sort of visionary experience.

Nowhere does Luke, or Paul, or anyone else work out the relationship between Paradise, resurrection, and God's dream for the world (the kingdom of God). It seems likely that the early Christians believed in some kind of intermediate state between death and resurrection. In Paul's letter to the Philippians, he speaks of death as a departing to be with Christ. Even though living in the earthly sphere was, for Paul, a living with and in Christ, departing in death to be with Christ evidently meant a new level of existence (Phil 1:21–24).

It would have been quite natural for the early disciples to call this next level of existence Paradise, recalling the garden in Genesis. In fact, in the Septuagint (the Greek translation of the Hebrew Bible), the Garden of Eden is called Paradise. In a hot, arid climate, a lush, fruitful, well-watered garden was an apt symbol for a flourishing life.

The mention of Paradise, however, is not the heart of the promise. Paradise is just a symbol. Jesus says, "Today, you will be *with me* in Paradise." Jesus is saying, "Wherever I am going, you are going, too. You will be with me where I am." What Jesus says to the criminal on the cross is very similar to the words he speaks to the disciples in John's Gospel: "In my Father's house there are many dwelling places. If it were not so, would I have told you that I go to prepare a place for you? And if I go and prepare a place for you, I will come again and will take you to myself, so that where I am, there you may be also" (John 14:2–3). However one interprets these words in John, *the key point the text makes is that the disciples will be with Jesus.* Paul says in his letter to the Romans that nothing, no power in heaven and earth, not even death, can separate us from the love of God that is in Christ Jesus, our Lord (Rom 8:38–39).

Undoubtedly, the word *today* has special significance. In Luke 4, Jesus enters the synagogue in Nazareth and reads from the prophet Isaiah: "The Spirit of the Lord is upon me, because he has anointed me to bring good news to the poor. He has sent me to proclaim release to the captives and recovery of sight to the blind, to let the oppressed go free, to proclaim the year of the Lord's favor" (Luke 4:18–19). Then after he rolls the scroll back up, with all eyes fastened on him, Jesus says, "Today, this scripture has been fulfilled in your hearing" (Luke 4:21). Today is the day the gospel goes out to the poor, the blind, the oppressed, and the prisoners (the insurrectionists, murderers, thieves), like these two hanging on the cross with Jesus.

No one is beyond hope; no one is beyond the pale. Even to the very powers that orchestrated his crucifixion and nailed him to the cross, Jesus said, "Father, forgive them for they do not know what they are doing." *It doesn't matter who you are or what you have done, today is the day of salvation. Today is the year, the month, the hour, the moment of the Lord's favor.*

Today is the day for a new beginning. Experiencing grace, the Lord's favor, doesn't mean that our circumstances will change. Maybe they will; maybe they won't. When someone you love dies, you can't bring them back. Some relationships that are broken cannot be restored, at least not to the way they were before they were broken. *The dying thief is dying on a cross with Jesus and there is no changing his inevitable death, but the word of promise and hope spoken by Jesus changes everything. It changes nothing and yet it changes everything.*

The grace of God mediated through Jesus comes to us full of potential and hope. One evening the Sci-fi channel was playing a movie based on Stephen King's book, *The Stand*. I caught it about halfway through. I picked up the story line fairly easily. It is a classic tale about the conflict between good and evil. There is a devil figure named Flag and a Savior figure—an elderly African-American woman known as Mother Abigail. A young man who is a deaf-mute and a member of the inner circle of disciples ends up playing a vital role in the defeat of evil. He is a person of integrity and the most compassionate one in the group.

In one scene, Mother Abigail is talking about God and the role this young man will play in accomplishing God's will. His friend speaks up and says, "But he doesn't believe in God." Mother Abigail, not surprised in the least, turns gently to the young deaf man and communicates to him directly, *"That's okay child, because God believes in you."* That is God's word to each one of us—today!

Occasionally, I will care for my granddaughter, Sophie, who (at the time of this writing) is one-year old. I usually arrive at her house early in the morning and keep her until her mother gets home around three o'clock. We have a good time. She leads, I follow. I already know my place. Whenever she lets me, I hold her close and say to her over and over, "Pappie loves Sophie." I'm determined that if she looks to me for nothing else in life, she will know that she is always loved. But no matter how much I declare and demonstrate my love, when her mother or father walks through the door, with that longing to hold their precious child in their arms, Sophie wakes up. Her eyes widen and she smiles and laughs. Her entire body and face registers delight.

I believe that we should respond in a similar way when we become attuned to the presence of God. *When we open ourselves to the Presence that is always present, even when we have done wrong and gone astray and know that we must enter the Presence with contrition and repentance, still we should take delight in our Abba, the All-Compassionate One.* Because God loves us, God believes in us and takes delight in us.

Both criminals on the cross were children of God. They both had made bad choices that brought them to this moment. One died in bitterness, cursing God and mocking Jesus. The other died in peace, hopeful that all was not lost.

Our good God, we delight in your Presence and give you thanks for the love manifested and expressed to us through the life, death, and resurrection of Jesus, our Lord. We confess our sins and failures, the ways we have hurt and wounded and put down one another. And we claim your forgiveness, even as we extend forgiveness to our sisters and brothers who have hurt us, and ask forgiveness from those we have offended. May we discover the joy and hope in you that you find in us. May we delight in you the way you delight in us. Amen.

His death was not a payment owed to God's honor, nor was it divine punishment that he suffered as a substitute for sinners. . . . Far from being an event organized for a divine requirement, his death reveals the nature of the forces of evil that opposed the rule of God. It poses a contrast between the attempt to coerce by violence under the rule of evil and the nonviolence of the rule of God as revealed and made visible by the life, death, and resurrection of Jesus.[4]

The truth that the cross of Christ embodies about us is certainly that we are loved by God, but that we are loved as prodigals, as problematic creatures, as beings whose alienation from God, from one another, from ourselves, and from the inarticulate creation is so great that we will accept love only on our terms, when it corresponds with our desire to be affirmed without asking of us that we become authentic and without requiring of us any depth of commitment comparable to the love that is being shown us.[5]

Thieves crucified on either side of Jesus showed two possible responses. One mocked Jesus' powerlessness: *A Messiah who can't even save himself?* The other recognized a different kind of power. Taking the risk of faith, he asked Jesus to "remember me when you come into your kingdom." No one else, except in mockery, had addressed Jesus as a king.

4. Weaver, *The Nonviolent Atonement*, 44.
5. Hall, *The Cross in our Context*, 102.

The dying thief saw more clearly than anyone else the nature of Jesus' kingdom.[6]

6. Yancey, *The Jesus I Never Knew*, 203–4.

4

A New Family

> Meanwhile, standing near the cross of Jesus were his mother, and his mother's sister, Mary the wife of Clopas, and Mary Magdalene. When Jesus saw his mother and the disciple whom he loved standing beside her, he said to his mother, "Woman, here is your son." Then he said to the disciple, "Here is your mother." And from that hour the disciple took her into his own home.
> John 19:25–27

JOHN'S GOSPEL is full of words and phrases that have multiple meanings and convey a rich symbolism. A number of interpreters argue that these words of Jesus from the cross to his mother and the beloved disciple[1] should be understood symbolically and theologically, rather than literally. Jesus had other blood brothers who had been present alongside his mother in Cana and they would have

---

1. The beloved disciple ("the disciple whom he loved") functions theologically in John's Gospel as the model disciple. Here he is at the cross, faithful to the end. In the other Gospel accounts, all the disciples desert Jesus.

naturally been the ones to care for their mother. In fact, assuming that Joseph had been dead for sometime, Jesus' mother would have been in their care. Jesus certainly wasn't at home seeing to it.[2]

Jesus' mother appears twice in the Gospel of John. She appears at the beginning and end of Jesus' ministry, at the wedding in Cana of Galilee and at the cross. These two scenes form a bracket around Jesus' ministry. At the wedding scene there is a foreboding of what is to come. When she asks him to do something to remedy the problem of running out of wine, Jesus says, "Woman, my hour has not yet come," alluding to the hour of his death.[3] *It seems that Jesus' pronouncement from the cross is not a reference to ordinary family relations, but to the nucleus of a new family that finds its center at the cross.*

I find it interesting that those who push and preach traditional family values never appeal to Jesus. They read from the household code in Ephesians or Colossians, or from the Pastoral Epistles, or they reference some Old Testament text, but they never read from the Gospels or quote Jesus.

Most of us simply ignore Jesus' hard sayings, not knowing what to make of them. In Matthew's Gospel, Jesus indicates how his message divides families. He says, "For I have

2. It has also been noted by interpreters that these words Jesus speaks to his mother closely resemble the formulas used for rites of adoption in the ancient world.

3. Jesus also addresses her as "woman" at the cross. This was not intended to be derogatory or degrading in any way. Jesus also addressed the woman of Samaria (4:21) and Mary Magdalene by this word (20:15). In each instance where this word is used, the woman's initial response to Jesus is one of incomprehension.

come to set a man against his father, and a daughter against her mother, and a daughter-in-law against her mother-in-law; and one's foes will be members of one's own household. Whoever loves father or mother or son or daughter more than me is not worthy of me" (Matt 10:35–37).

Another time, the Gospels tell us that Jesus' mother and brothers came to try to talk him in to going home with them. They thought he had lost his good sense. They could see where his current course was taking him. They could see an inevitable clash with the dominating powers of the religious establishment and that could only mean one thing: Jesus would lose.

While Jesus is teaching a crowd, his family arrives. When Jesus is informed of their presence and that they are inquiring about him, he says, "'Who are my mother and brothers?' And looking at those who sat around him, he said, 'Here are my mother and my brothers! Whoever does the will of God is my brother and sister and mother'" (Mark 3:31–35).

Still another time, Jesus called a man to be his disciple whose father had just died. He wanted to bury his father. Jesus said, "Let the dead bury the dead, follow me" (Matt 8:22).

What are we to make of these sayings? About the only thing that makes sense is that Jesus had a larger vision and mission.[4] *Jesus envisioned a beloved community, the family of God, as constituting the core of the kingdom of God, God's*

4. It may also be true that Jesus was ministering with a sense of urgency. This is debated by scholars, but he may have believed that the full realization of God's reign/kingdom was imminent.

dream for the world. Jesus' commitment to this greater cause took precedence and priority over his own family.

For us it's just the opposite. I admit, I'm not like Jesus in this area, and I suspect that you are not either. Most of us give preference to our own families. That's pretty much a given in our culture, and very few of us are able to embrace the possibility of the beloved community as Jesus envisioned.

The first community of disciples as depicted by Luke in the book of Acts comes very close. Some interpreters think Luke's description is more ideal than real. I'm not sure. Consider his description,

> They devoted themselves to the apostles' teaching and fellowship, to the breaking of bread and the prayers. Awe came upon everyone, because many wonders and signs were being done by the apostles. All who believed were together and had all things in common; they would sell their possessions and goods and distribute the proceeds to all, as any had need. Day by day, as they spent much time together in the temple, they broke bread at home and ate their food with glad and generous hearts, praising God and having the goodwill of all the people. And day by day the Lord added to their number those who were being saved. Acts 2:42–47

I've told my kids, "What's mine is yours." But I haven't told any of my church members that.

I think that a healthy Christian spirituality will always hold in tension the radical demands of discipleship on one hand, and the radical grace of God on the other hand. It's good to know that our failures at discipleship are met with grace, isn't it?

Will Willimon is now a Bishop in the United Methodist Church. For many years he was a chaplain to students and professor at Duke University. He says that in twenty years as chaplain to the students, he received maybe ten or twelve angry telephone calls from parents. Never did they say, "Help! I sent my child to the university and he got addicted to alcohol," or "Help! I sent my child to college and she became sexually promiscuous." No, says Willimon. The calls he received were always, "Help! I sent my child to Duke and she became a religious fanatic." Religious fanatic defined as, "she's going on a two year mission to Haiti with the Catholics." Willimon says, "Give these parents credit. They know enough about Jesus to know that he creates havoc in a family."

During his last graduation weekend as campus minister, he told a young woman who was a graduating senior and an active participant in their campus ministry that he wanted to meet her parents. She didn't think that was a good idea. When he inquired, he was informed that her mother was really ticked off with him. She said, "She's flipped out because I'm thinking about going to work with the poor. She liked the old me that she once had better than the new me who's working with Jesus."[5]

In Luke's Gospel, when Mary and Joseph bring their child to the old prophet Simeon in the temple for his blessing, he predicts that the child "is destined for the falling and rising of many in Israel." Then he warns Mary, "and a sword will pierce your own soul too" (Luke 2:34–35). Jesus

5. Willimon, *Thank God It's Friday*, 30–31, 33.

broke the heart of his mother, and has divided many a family since.

The call of Jesus is a call to embrace a larger family and a greater cause than a single family can sustain. When Jesus talked about the kingdom of God he did not envisage a conquering, domineering empire, but a loving, caring household. And at the center of this household is the family of God, the beloved community.

When the church is at its best it inspires us to embrace a larger family and cause, and to exemplify this in our worship, fellowship, spirituality, and ministry. We are called to manifest and embody the love of Christ to each other and to our world. Sometimes we become so absorbed in the church's institutional life that we forget what the church is and what it is called to do.

Some readers will recall the verse they learned as a kid, along with the accompanying hand motions: "Here is the church and here is the steeple, open it up and see all the people." That's terrible ecclesiology (a fancy word for the doctrine or theology of the church). That little ditty implies that the church is the building where the people gather. No, the church is the people; the building is simply where the church gathers to worship and share life together. *We who are followers of Jesus constitute the church, bound together by a covenant of discipleship to Jesus, our Lord, sealed by his death (Mark 14:22–25).* We are bound together both universally and locally. As a local community, a church forms a small cell in the beloved community of God's new world. The church is called to embody (incarnate) the life of God's new world, God's new creation.

Our blood families are too narrowly restricted and confined to launch us and sustain us in our larger commitment to God's kingdom on earth. In the church we learn that we are connected and tied to a larger group of "sisters and brothers" with whom we may have no natural affinity. I like Willimon's take on this,

> So one thing the church does for us in baptism is to adopt us, to rescue us from the ravages of a society that asks too much from its families, that puts too much weight on family values, in order to place us in a new family that's over two thousand years old with millions upon millions of brothers and sisters, living and dead. The church gives us more important work to do in life than merely sacrifice and take and give from people who look exactly like us.[6]

In the later chapters of the book of Romans, Paul gives some wonderful teaching on what it means to be the family of God. In Seminary, I took a Greek exegesis class on the book of Romans. We spent almost the whole class time on chapters 1–8. Then, as the class started to wind down, we hurried through chapters 9–11, and had to completely skip over chapters 12–16. That was terrible class management. Too often it is assumed that the later chapters in Romans are sort of an appendix, an addendum to the epistle, and not really that important.

That, I think, is a misreading of Romans. A number of modern interpreters contend that the final chapters of Romans constitute the crux and climax of Paul's presentation of the gospel. The final chapters are absolutely vital

6. Ibid., 33.

because they show us what all the theological language Paul uses at the beginning of the letter means.

In the earlier part of the letter, Paul talks about justification, the putting right, the restoring of right relations with God, with one another, and with all creation. In the later chapters, Paul spells out what that means in the life of the church. In the first part of the letter, Paul talks about dying with Christ to the reign of sin, and living in the power of the Spirit, which is the power of the new age, the power of the risen Christ. In the later chapters, Paul shows us what that looks like and how life in the Spirit is expressed. These final chapters in Romans constitute the most important part of the book.

Consider this passage from Romans 15,

> We who are strong ought to put up with the failings of the weak, and not to please ourselves. Each of us must please our neighbor for the good purpose of building up the neighbor. For Christ did not please himself; but, as it is written, "The insults of those who insult you have fallen on me." For whatever was written in former days was written for our instruction, so that by steadfastness and by the encouragement of the scriptures we might have hope. May the God of steadfastness and encouragement grant you to live in harmony with one another, in accordance with Jesus Christ. So that together you may with one voice glorify the God and Father of our Lord Jesus Christ. Welcome one another, therefore, just as Christ has welcomed you, for the glory of God. Romans 15:1–7

This is what it means to live out our justification, to live in covenant faithfulness to God and each other. This is what it means to live in the power of the Spirit. And this is what it means to be the church, to be the family of God. The strong bear the failings of the weak, thinking of the well-being of others, rather than themselves. Each member strives to please his or her neighbor for the purpose of building up the neighbor, helping one's brother or sister grow and become more. *The church strives, not for uniformity in doctrine and practice, but for unity in love for one another. The church accepts each person unconditionally just as Christ accepts each one.* This, according to Paul, is part of what it means to be the family of God.

It's not easy to live this way. It takes discipline and practice. We will certainly fall short and miss the mark, which is why the cross is so central to our life together. *The family of God is formed at the foot of the cross. The cross speaks of forgiveness and suffering. When we walk in the way of the cross, we bear one another's sins and suffer with one another and forgive one another for the many ways we fail to live up to our covenant obligations to be a sister and brother to our sisters and brothers.*

Flannery O'Conner lived for a time alone and unknown in New York. She said that going to church in such an impersonal setting had its advantages. Upon returning from Mass at a fairly prominent church, she commented on her experience, "Although you see several people you wish you knew, you see thousands you're glad you don't know."[7]

That's not church. This may be, though, the appeal of the mega-church to some people. One can slide in and out

7. Ibid., 35.

without anyone really noticing. One can take it all in without ever having to give anything out. It's possible to go to church all our lives, and never really be the church.

We need to be stuck with people that we would not choose to be with otherwise. We need to be able to accept them as our sisters and brothers and take on the responsibility of being a brother or sister or mother or father. We need this in order to learn how to love our neighbor as our self. We need the church in order to learn how to be sisters and brothers and mothers and fathers to one another, just as much as the world needs to see us being God's new family.

On the cross Jesus says, "Woman, here is your son." And to the beloved disciple he says, "Here is your mother." The community gathers around the cross. As we take up our cross, as we bear the sins of others through forgiveness, as we die to our ego and selfishness, as we give ourselves to others the way Jesus gave even unto death, we become the beloved community, we lead the way into God's kingdom.

Our gracious God, you have brought us together as sisters and brothers, mothers and fathers in your family, to show us how to accept, bear with, care for, forgive, and love one another. Forgive us our failures at loving one another the way you love us, and help to grow and become the family that you long for us to be. Amen.

Community is like a large mosaic. Each little piece seems so insignificant. One piece is bright red, another cold blue or dull green, another warm purple, another sharp yellow, another shining gold. Some look precious, others ordinary. Some look valuable, other worthless. Some look gaudy, others delicate. As individual stones, we can do little with them except compare them and judge their beauty and value. When, however, all these little stones are brought together in one big mosaic portraying the face of Christ, who would ever question the importance of any one of them? If one of them, even the least spectacular one, is missing, the face is incomplete. Together in the one mosaic, each little stone is indispensable and makes a unique contribution to the glory of God. That's community, a fellowship of little people who together make God visible in the world.[8]

The Holy Spirit creates HOLY community. "All those who are led by the Spirit of God are sons and daughters of God" (Romans 8:14). This means that all who live in harmony with the divine dynamics at work in nature and in history constitute the community called CHURCH. It is for those people we must look—both inside and outside the institutional churches—if we want to find the HOLY CHURCH. This phrase of the [The Apostles'] Creed does not assert that a particular institution called "church" is holy—that it manifests divine life. Rather it is the other way around: wherever divine life manifests itself in community we are in the presence of CHURCH, the *Ecclesia*, the community of those who follow the call of the Spirit.[9]

Community is a place of forgiveness. In spite of all the trust we may have in each other, there are always words that wound, self-promoting attitudes, situations where susceptibilities clash. That is why living together implies a cross, a constant effort, an acceptance which is daily, and mutual forgiveness . . . To forgive is to recognize once again—after

8. Nouwen, *The Essential Henry Nouwen*, 143.

9. Steindl-Rast, *Deeper Than Words*, 139.

separation—the covenant which binds us together with those we do not get along with well; it is to be open and listening to them once again. It is to give them space in our hearts. That is why it is never easy to forgive. We too must change. We must learn to forgive and forgive and forgive every day, day after day. We need the power of the Holy Spirit in order to open up like that.[10]

10. Vanier, *Community and Growth*, 37–38.

5

Thirsting for Life

> After this, when Jesus knew that all was now fin-
> ished, he said (in order to fulfill the scripture), "I
> am thirsty." John 19:28

THE EARLY disciples of Jesus, convinced that God raised
him from the dead and that through his life, death, resurrection, and living presence, God acted and continues to
act to save the world, began to develop beliefs with regard to
Jesus' nature and his relation to God. The attempt to understand and describe the nature of Jesus and his relationship
with God is called Christology. John's Gospel has a very
high Christology. John's Gospel assumes that Jesus is divine,
and his divinity is often read back into the stories. John's
high Christology guides the way John tells the story of Jesus
and is most certainly behind the ways in which John shapes
and reformulates the sayings of Jesus into lengthy dialogues
and monologues. Sometimes in John's narrative the divinity
of Jesus trumps his humanity.

This brief word of Jesus from the cross is a case in point.
Jesus' expression, "I am thirsty," reflects a very human Jesus.

But in introducing these words, John presents Jesus as being in complete control, intentionally fulfilling Scripture.[1] John's picture is very different from the portrait painted in Mark's Gospel of a Jesus who is mostly passive and cries out, echoing the words of the Psalmist, "My God, my God, why have you forsaken me?" There is no sense of abandonment and forsakenness in John's passion story.

I pointed out in the last chapter that John's Gospel thrives on symbolical and double meanings. *The words here may indeed have a deeper meaning: Jesus' thirst is to do the will of God, even if it involves suffering and death. Disciples of Jesus acquire that same thirst.* A significant aspect of what it means to be thirsty is reflected in an earlier passage in John's Gospel,

> On the last day of the festival, the great day, while Jesus was standing there, he cried out, "Let anyone who is thirsty come to me, and let the one who believes in me drink. As the scripture has said, 'Out of the believer's heart shall flow rivers of living water.'" Now he said this about the Spirit, which believers in him were to receive; for as yet there was no Spirit, because Jesus was not yet glorified. John 7:37–39

Jesus is able to quench our thirst for "life" by providing "living water" that flows from within. Here John interprets

1. All the Gospels emphasize the fulfillment of Scripture in the passion story, but John does this more than the others. The reference here seems to be to Psalm 69:22, which in the LXX contains the same Greek words John uses for "sour wine" and "thirst." Sometimes the connections the Gospel writers make with the Hebrew text are finely stretched. It was their way of emphasizing that God was at work in and through these events.

the metaphor. The living water refers to the spiritual life mediated through the Spirit of the living Christ, which was poured out on Jesus' followers after his resurrection/glorification.

The spiritual life of the living Christ quenches our thirst in a variety of ways. One of the primary ways, I think, is in our quest for meaning and purpose. *The thirst for meaning and purpose is inseparably tied to other thirsts, such as the thirst for real community of mutual caring, sharing, and healing. The thirst for meaning is also connected to the passion for justice for all people, where inequities are corrected, wrongs made right, and no one is marginalized, excluded, or taken advantage of.* One of Jesus' beatitudes in Matthew's Gospel pronounces a blessing on those who hunger and thirst for distributive, restorative justice (Matt 5:6).

In *Death of a Salesman,* Willie Loman spends his life in pursuit of being a successful salesman. He lives with the illusion that if he can be successful in his work, his life will be fulfilled. He doesn't have the courage to face his failures or to ask the critical question if what he was pursuing had real meaning. In the end, he commits suicide. His son, Biff, says to a friend, "There were a lot of nice days. When he'd come home from a trip; or on Sundays, making the stoop; finishing the cellar; putting on the new porch. . . . You know something, Charley, there's more of him in that front stoop than in all the sales he ever made. . . . He had the wrong dreams. All, all wrong. . . . He never knew who he was."[2] Disciples of Jesus discover who they are through a relationship with Christ.

2. Miller, *The Death of a Salesman,* 138.

To thirst is to be alive; the dead do not get thirsty. Those who are spiritually alive thirst for the "more"—the Transcendent, The Really Real, the Ultimate Reality. For those of us who are Christians, it is a thirst for the reality of the living Christ. We look to Christ to bring coherence, meaning, and balance to life.

We discover in our relationship to Christ a life that exudes faith and hope, that assimilates his wisdom and teachings, and that expresses his grace and truth. We learn from Christ how to love one another, the creation, and God. We find real purpose in pursuing God's dream for the world as proclaimed and embodied by Jesus in the Gospels. *As we learn to live in reliance upon the Spirit of the living Christ, we discover real meaning oriented around a growing intention and will to love as Christ loved.*

On the fifth day of their six-day climb up Kilimanjaro in 2002, Dr. Frank Artress awoke early, while his wife Susan Gustafson was still sleeping. The twenty-two African porters were just beginning to stir. Artress wanted to do something big for his fiftieth birthday. He was an amateur photographer with a new Nikon, so he began photographing the sun rising over the snow at sixteen thousand feet.

He knew his drinking water was frozen, but figured it would melt during the all-day hike up the steep rocky face to Crater Camp where they would spend the night, before summiting the next morning. The group trekked all day, but Artress' water did not thaw. Embarrassed, he didn't tell anyone how thirsty he was. After they stopped for lunch, he began to lose his breath. His lungs started to slowly fill with fluid.

He turned to his wife and said, "We are in a really, really bad place." As a cardiac anesthesiologist, he knew the signs of high altitude pulmonary edema. The only cure was to descend, but the route they had taken was too rocky and dangerous to descend, especially at night. The only option was to make the eight hundred and forty-foot climb to the top and go back down the other side.

Artress led his wife to a rock and they sat together above the clouds, holding each other and crying. He wasn't afraid to die, but he was ashamed. He had lived only for himself—practicing medicine in a Modesto hospital, traveling with his wife, purchasing luxury vacation homes and collecting art. He felt as if he had nothing to show for his fifty years. He felt as if his life had been a waste. He thought how stupid it would be to die without ever giving anything back to society.

By midnight, Artress was concerned that he wouldn't make it. Shivering under a pile of blankets he told his wife, "We've got to do something, or I'm going to be dead by morning." His wife roused up the camp, and they set off in the darkness for the summit. It took eight hours to climb the eight hundred and forty feet to the top. Their guide Kitaba and the porters wrapped arms around Frank and sang Swahili songs to encourage him.

They made it down the other side to a ranger station where he passed out. When he awoke, he was in a sleeping bag, strapped to a military cot with a motorcycle tire under it. Four porters were each holding a corner and running down the mountain, still singing Swahili prayer songs. These men who barely knew Artress had risked their own lives, climbing in the darkness, to save his. Artress was overwhelmed with gratitude.

Kitaba was able to get Artress to a doctor in a clinic the next day. The doctor saw no heart damage. On his way out, the doctor, a U.S.-trained Australian, said to Artress, "You know, Dr. Frank, we need doctors here in Africa way more than they need them in California."

That night Frank and Susan stayed up late talking about how to live a life of purpose. What better way to thank the people who had saved his life than by returning to their medically deprived village so he could save theirs?

When they returned to Modesto, they quit their jobs and sold everything—the Montana ranch, the condos in Colorado and Palm Springs, the forty-thousand-dollar garden sculptures. All the things that they once put such great value on had now lost their appeal. It all looked like "junk," they said.

Their new African home was a tiny apartment on one of the noisiest streets in Arusha. Their electricity was intermittent, their tap water brown, their showers cold. They learned to like goat meat. And they were at peace.

At the clinic, Artress saw everything. It amounted to a crash course in tropical diseases. It was like being in a residency program all over again. He saw children with bugs in their ears and foot-long worms in their intestines. Many of his patients walked days to see him. Most people in northern Tanzania have a life expectancy of less than forty years, succumbing most often to malaria, tuberculosis and routine infections from drinking water. The heartbreak of Africa, says Dr. Artress, is that people don't have access to even the most basic care. He relies on a well-thumbed reference book, *Tropical Medicine and Emerging Infectious Diseases*, and the internet. He emails experts in America about bizarre cases.

In 2005 they bought a twenty-foot Mitsubishi bus, with four-wheel drive, running water, and oxygen. They added solar electricity. They pass out antibiotics, vitamins, and bandages. From the back of the bus they give malaria tests and sew up cuts. It's a mobile clinic.

In 2004 they formed a charity called FAME— The Foundation for African Medicine and Education. Construction has begun on a forty-room hospital in Karatu, a city of one hundred eighty-thousand. When construction is complete it will be the first hospital in the city. Sometimes Dr. Frank and Susan are overwhelmed by the gratitude of the people who see him as some kind of angel who has come to them with medicine. Now when he is at death's door these are the people he will think about.[3]

Jesus said that he did not come to do his own will, but the will of the One who sent him. His thirst for meaning was fulfilled in being God's agent for healing and redemption. Jesus tells his disciples, "As the Father sent me, so I send you." *When we join the living Spirit of Christ and the Father and Mother of all creation in the healing and restoring of life, in loving and serving and caring for all God's children, our thirst for meaning is satisfied.*

Our good God, some of us have thirsts that we have tried to fulfill in selfish ways. We have attempted to satisfy these cravings in ways and means that have been destructive and detrimental to the health and well-being of others, as well as

---

3. See the story links at www.fameafrica.org.

*our own lives. We have indulged, exploited, and arrogantly
asserted our will above your will and the good of the creation.
And we are ashamed. Give us, O Lord, a vision of how we
might invest our lives in meaningful ways and participate
with you in your project to heal, renew, and reconcile all
things to yourself and to one another. May healing grace and
unconditional love flow from within us out to others like
streams of living water. May our thirst for life be quenched as
we give our lives to enhance the lives of others. Amen.*

Jesus sends the Spirit so that we may be led to the full truth
of the divine life. *Truth* does not mean an idea, concept, or
doctrine, but the true relationship. To be led into the truth
is to be led into the same relationship that Jesus has with
the Father . . . Pentecost is the completion of Jesus' mission.
On Pentecost the fullness of Jesus' ministry becomes visible. When the Holy Spirit descends upon the disciples and
dwells with them, their lives are transformed into Christ-
like lives, lives shaped by the same love that exists between
the Father and the Son. The spiritual life is indeed a life in
which we are lifted up to become partakers of the divine
life.[4]

The Holy Spirit is that aspect of God that works largely from
within and "secretly," at "the deepest levels of our desiring,"
as so many of the mystics have said. That's why the mystical
tradition could only resort to subtle metaphors like wind,
fire, descending doves, and flowing water to describe the
Spirit. More than anything else, the Spirit keeps us connected and safely inside an already existing flow, if we but
allow it. We never "create" or earn the Spirit; we discover

4. Nouwen, *Making All Things New*, 54.

this inner abiding as we learn to draw upon our deepest inner life. . . . The Holy Spirit is always entirely for us, more than we are for ourselves, it seems. She speaks in our favor against the negative voices that judge and condemn us. . . . True spirituality is always a deep "co-operating" (Romans 8:28) between the two [the soul and God]. True spirituality is a kind of *synergy* in which both parties give and both parties receive to create one shared truth and joy.[5]

I believe that the aspiration for peace, communion, and universal love is greater and deeper in people than the need to win in the competition of life. But for this aspiration to become a real desire that inspires our activities, in order for it to break through our fears and the need to win, each one of us has to make a leap into trust: trust in the sacredness of every human heart, trust in the beauty of the universe, trust that in working for peace and unity, and in purging our false self, we will find a treasure.[6]

5. Rohr, *Falling Upward*, 90, 92.
6. Vanier, *Becoming Human*, 123.

6

The Glory of Love

A jar full of sour wine was standing there. So
they put a sponge full of the wine on a branch of
hyssop and held it to his mouth. When Jesus had
received the wine, he said, "It is finished." Then
he bowed his head and gave up his spirit. John
19:29

IN THE movie *Ray*, Ray Charles had two recurring dreams
that replayed two pivotal experiences. In one, he was a
boy of seven, just turning blind. His mother Aretha says
to him, "Always remember your promise to me. Never let
nobody or nothing turn you into no cripple." Though he
was a trusting child, he soon learned to trust no one. His
father was nowhere around and Ray seemed to hook up
with people who continually looked for opportunities to
take advantage of him. He learned to depend on his wits,
his ears, and his musical abilities.

Another dream that haunted Ray was the death of his
brother, George. George was a child, maybe four or five,
when he died. His mother was doing the wash, and the
boys were running through the clean sheets hanging in the

yard, playing tag. George said that he didn't want to play any more and moved off in another direction. He climbed the table where his mother's large wash tub sat full of water. He tripped, fell backwards, and landed in the water. Ray first thought George was fooling around, then stared, dazed and frozen, as George thrashed around and suddenly lay silent. Seeing George's feet motionless in the tub, Aretha races to him and tries to revive him. She holds him tight as she looks at Ray and says, "Why didn't you do something? Why didn't you call me?" At the funeral, Ray watches his mom throw herself on the casket, beside herself with grief.

He was on the road constantly. He had affairs with his lead singers. From 1950 to 1965 he was on drugs. In the scene where he started his drug habit, Fathead and another band member were doing heroin. Ray wanted in. Fathead said, "You don't want this, Ray. This ain't weed, Ray. It's the null and void." Ray retorted, "Null and void, just like my life. I'll be right at home."

In 1965 he was arrested for possession. Out on bail and at home, he felt a craving just as he was getting in a fight with his wife of eleven years, Della Bea. She confronts him, "No, Ray, no! A needle ain't gonna solve this!"

"Get out of the way! Move!"

"Only thing that can help you is God, Ray."

"Don't you talk about God! Do you have any idea how it feels to go blind and still be afraid of the dark? And every day, you sit there and pray for just a little light, and you get nothing, 'cause God don't listen to people like me."

"Stop talking like that."

"As far as I'm concerned, me and God is even and I do what I please. And Goddamn it, if I want to shoot up, I shoot up." Della Bea threatens to take the boys and leave.

"You know I love you and those boys more than anything."

"No, that is a damn lie, and you know it!" She mentions the little league banquet that Ray missed, when his son won most valuable player. He was too loaded. "No, there is something you love more than me and them boys, more than all the women you ever slept with on the road, more than all the dope you ever took. Your music. And if you don't stop using that needle, they're gonna take away your music, and put you in jail. Is that poison worth losing everything?"

Later, Ray spends a number of weeks as a patient at St. Francis Rehabilitation Clinic where he finally gets off heroin. In one scene he is playing chess with his psychiatrist, who praises him for his progress. Ray says, "I'm done with this dope and I'm finished."

The psychiatrist asks him, "Who is George?" Ray pauses, then says, "Forget the head shrinking, Doc. I can handle this." The doctor tells him that he is far from being whole, that he can't help him if he is unwilling to talk, and then leaves the room. Ray, in anger, gets up and goes after the doctor, tripping on a chair.

As he falls, he has another flashback, only this one is different. He falls into the wash bucket, where he gropes for George, but he's not there. He turns, seeing the colored bottles hanging on the tree outside his boyhood home. His mother is there.

"Talk to me, son."

"Mama, I kept my promise."

"You got strong all right. Went places I never dreamed of. But you still became a cripple." Ray wept. "Come here, baby. Come here."

As Ray weeps, he hears a voice. "Ray?" He turns and sees George. "It wasn't your fault." They hug.

"Now promise us, you never let nobody or nothing turn you into no cripple ever again. That you'll always stand on your own two feet."

"I promise."

From that day, Ray never touched heroin again.

Many of us, like Ray, look through lenses clouded by fear, insecurity, guilt, bitterness, resentment, and anger; through these lenses we see an ungracious world. We repeat grievance stories of unforgiveness, hurt, and pain inflicted upon us and that we have inflicted on others—stories of rejection, exclusion, and condemnation. Seeing an ungracious world, we become hardened by ungraciousness. We look at life devoid of generosity, forgiveness, and hope.

To live in a world of ungraciousness—alienated from God and one another—is to live in a spiritual state of death. For many years, Ray lived in a state of death, a world of ungrace, a world of "null and void."

We have all been profoundly shaped and influenced by things that have happened over which we had no control. Ray could not help that his father ran out on the family. He could not have prevented his brother's death. He could not halt the blindness that overtook him. There is much in life over which we have no control—our genetics, family of origin, early childhood experiences, the culture we grow up in, influences and events tied to time and place, as well as many other factors. Yet, at some point we have to assume responsibility for our lives with whatever degree of freedom we have. In spite of all that happened to Ray, he still had choices. We have choices.

If we are to move from a state of death into life and begin to live in a gracious world, we must take responsibility for the choices we do have. The Gospel of John calls this faith, which is much more than intellectual assent to certain beliefs. Faith is largely about putting on new eyeglasses with which to see the world, so that we begin to see the love and grace of God that is present and operative in the world.

We must stop lying to ourselves and others. We must stop evading the truth about ourselves; stop deluding ourselves about why we need to grasp and gain power and use our position and power to take advantage of others. Like Ray Charles, who was both a victim and a victimizer, we get used and then we use others to get what we want. *The first step toward a flourishing life in God's gracious world is our admission of complicity in an ungracious world.*

How do we do that? We can look to Jesus, particularly Jesus on the cross who says, "It is finished." As the serpent on the staff was lifted up by Moses in the camp of Israel, and everyone who looked upon it found healing, so everyone who looks in faith to Jesus lifted up on the cross can find healing and new life (John 3:14–15).

At the cross, the worlds of ungrace and grace collide; the powers of death and life meet with explosive force. As Jesus anticipates his death he says, "Now is the judgment of the world (the Domination System), now the ruler of the world will be driven out" (12:31). The ruler of the world, mythical or real, is the representative, the epitome of the power of evil and hate that crucified Jesus. This is the power that entered into the heart of Judas (13:2) and why he is called a devil (6:70). Jesus, as the light of the world, exposed the world's darkness, and because the System loved darkness more than light, the world determined to destroy the light.[1]

The irony is that in the very act of destroying the light, the darkness of the System is exposed and the light casts its radiance against the darkness in a ray of glory. *The irony of the cross is that while this horrible event is the final act of hostility against Jesus by the powers of evil, it is also the final act of Jesus in revealing God's magnanimous love for the world.* The crucifixion reflects both the culmination of hostility against Jesus and the climax of God's revelation of love for the world through Jesus.

This horrendous outpouring of hate, resulting in the torture and suffering of Jesus, becomes a redemptive event in which the love of God engages and defeats the forces of evil. *God defeats it, not by returning evil for evil, hate for hate, blow for blow, but by bearing, absorbing, and exhausting it. This is how the Lamb of God takes away the sin of the world* (John 1:29, 36).[2] In John, the reference is to sin (singular), not sins—the sin of hate that issues in violence. The deadly and destructive nature of violence, prejudice, and

1. This is cosmic theater, depicting the clash between good and evil as the clash between the world/the Devil and Christ.

2. John's Gospel interprets Jesus' death through the Passover imagery. Jesus' ministry is framed by Passovers. Jesus' death corresponds to the time of the death of the Passover lambs in preparation for the commemorative evening meal (19:14). Jesus is slain at the same time the Passover lambs are slain. Christ is being depicted as the new liberator. The cross points toward a new exodus. Jesus leads his followers out of death into life.

hate is exposed at the cross. The capacity to see evil as evil is the first step in overcoming evil. But it is an overcoming through love, not hate.

There must be, however, a lure, a compelling reason, insight, or motivation to abandon evil, and so the cross functions, not only as a revelation of our sin (our hate that issues in violence), but as a revelation of God's love. *The cross is the lure, drawing us to a loving God where the power of love resides.* The cross, then, becomes the means of our liberation from the power of sin and death. It becomes our Exodus, a redemptive event, through which we pass from death to life as the children of Israel passed from the bondage of slavery into freedom. As we enter into Jesus' experience on the cross through faith, as God's love is poured out in our hearts, we find the power to bear the hate, prejudice, and evil of the world.

Christ becomes our liberator, rescuing us from the debilitating forces within our souls that would shackle us in bitterness, malice, and hate. Christ becomes in our actual experience our brother in the family of God, our friend and comrade on the journey of life and partner in the work of the kingdom of God.

The cross, then, is Jesus' concluding work. It is Jesus completing (finishing) the work God gave him to do (17:4). It is the crowning event that will eventually draw all people to Christ (12:32). This is why, in John's Gospel, the death of Jesus is consistently referred to as both Jesus' glorification and the glorification of God. Speaking of his death Jesus says, "The hour has come for the Son of Man to be glorified" (12:23). It is because the cross reveals the magnitude and expansiveness of God's love for the world that it can be referred to as Jesus' glorification or the glorification of God.[3] *Christ descended to the darkest place to die a shameful, horrible death, and yet here is where the love of God for the world shines the brightest.*

Once we see our complicity in the crucifixion, that we are not just victims but victimizers, then we are ready to experience an exodus from hate into forgiveness and love. We admit first, that while bad things may have happened to us beyond our control, we have, nevertheless, hardened our hearts and chosen to live in an ungracious world. We know that the powers of hate that crucified Jesus reside in us. Once we find the courage to make that good confession, then we are ready to behold God's love at the cross and experience its liberating power. The cross then becomes a model for us: "This is my commandment, that you love one another as I have loved you. No one has greater love than this, to lay down one's life for one's friends" (15:12–13).

When we unite with Jesus on the cross, we draw from his Spirit and find the inner resolve and grace to give up hate and the need for revenge. We pass through the waters of condemnation without the need or want to condemn in return, and we determine to allow love to grow and flourish into gratitude and generosity. Jesus called this being born again, and we need to be born again and again and again as we cast off the works of this ungracious world and increasingly manifest the fruit of the Spirit. In an exodus through

3. In the OT the "glory" of God was sometimes equated with the presence of God; usually, the manifest presence of God. In John's Gospel, Jesus is the quintessential mediator of the divine presence. The miracles are called "signs" in John because they signify spiritual truth and reveal God's glory (see 2:11). In one sense, the cross is the sign that reveals the glory of God's love.

the cross we leave behind a world of selfish grasping and grinding egoism, and enter a vibrant and abundant world of grace.

Help us, O Lord, as your daughters and sons, to renew our commitment to live in the world of grace, where justice and mercy kiss each other, where forgiveness is the air we breathe, and compassion is the water we drink. We give thanks for the magnitude of your love revealed in all its glory at the cross. As we admit to the darkness within our souls, may the light of your love dispel the darkness of all hate and evil, filling us with grace and truth. Amen

In the book of Numbers, Yahweh tells Moses to raise up a serpent on a standard, and "anyone who has been bitten by a serpent and looks upon it will be healed" (21:8). The very thing that was killing them is the thing that will heal them! I would ask you to consider the crucifix as a *homeopathic* image, like those medicines that give you just enough of the disease so you could develop a resistance and be healed from it. *The cross dramatically reveals the problem of ignorant killing, to inoculate us against doing the same thing.* Salvation history seems to lead people into the very darkness that they seek to overcome. There they learn its real character, and how to unlock it from the inside. John sees it as what Jesus is doing on the cross (John 3:13; 8:28; 12:31; 19:37).[4]

Those who "gaze upon" (John 19:37) the crucified long enough—with contemplative eyes—are always healed at deep levels of pain, unforgiveness, aggressivity, and

4. Rohr, *Things Hidden*, 191.

victimhood. It demands no theological education at all, just an "inner exchange" by receiving the image and offering one's soul back in safe return. . . . The mystery of the rejection, suffering, passion, death and raising up of Jesus is *the interpretative key* for what history means and where it is going. . . . *If all these human crucifixions are leading to some possible resurrection, and are not dead-end tragedies, this changes everything. If God is somehow participating in human suffering, instead of just passively tolerating it and observing it*, that also changes everything—at least for those who are willing to "gaze" contemplatively.[5]

Jesus takes away the sin of the world by dramatically exposing what is the real sin of the world (ignorant attacking and killing, not purity codes), by refusing the usual pattern of attacking and killing back, and, in fact, "returning their curses with blessings" (Luke 6:27), then finally by teaching us that we can "follow him" in doing the same. . . . Like most spiritual things, it cannot be understood with any dualistic or rational mind, but only at the level of soul. It is a transformational image and message that utterly rearranges one's reality and idea of the very nature of God. *Evil is not overcome by attack or even avoidance, but by union at a higher level. It is overcome not by fight or flight, rather by "fusion"!*[6]

---

5. Ibid., 186.
6. Ibid., 188–87.

7

Why Call Friday Good?

It was now about noon, and darkness came over the whole land until three in the afternoon, while the sun's light failed; and the curtain of the temple was torn in two. Then Jesus, crying with a loud voice said, "Father, into your hands I commend my spirit." Having said this, he breathed his last. When the centurion saw what had taken place, he praised God and said, "Certainly this man was innocent." And when all the crowds who had gathered there for this spectacle saw what had taken place, they returned home, beating their breasts. But all his acquaintances, including the women who had followed him from Galilee, stood at a distance, watching these things. Luke 23:44–49

THESE WORDS of Jesus in Luke's Gospel, "Father, into your hands I commend my spirit," are equivalent to Jesus' words in John's Gospel, "It is finished." In telling the Passion Story, the Gospels of Mark and Matthew include only one saying of Jesus from the cross: His cry of abandonment, "My

God, my God, why have you forsaken me?" The other six sayings of Jesus are found in Luke and John.

In Mark and Matthew, the emphasis is on Jesus as a participant in our suffering. Jesus shares our pain and loss. Jesus knows what it is like to feel forsaken, even by God. Jesus, for the most part, is a passive victim. In Luke and John, Jesus is still a victim, but he is not passive. There is no sense of Jesus feeling forsaken in Luke or John. In Luke's portrait, Jesus dies as a courageous and faithful martyr.

We need both portraits. We need to know that God suffers with us, that God identifies with our experiences of forsakenness and feelings of abandonment, that God joins us in our rejection and humiliation. But we also need to know that neither Jesus nor God was surprised by the crucifixion, and that God incorporated Jesus' death into God's redemptive plan. In Luke, Jesus is the overcoming victim, offering his life sacrificially.

By sacrifice I do not mean that Jesus died to appease God's wrath, or satisfy God's justice, or pay some debt owed to God. I do not mean that Jesus bore a penalty imposed by God. Jesus did not die to save us from God. We do not need to be saved from God. We need to be saved from our sins, from the hate, greed, prejudice, and violence that have roots in every human heart and found collective expression through the religious and political powers that killed Jesus.

The Apostle Paul and many of the early Christians used sacrificial imagery to talk about the significance of Jesus' death, but they never attempted to explain the imagery. The New Testament employs several different metaphors drawn from the cultic life and worship of Judaism. The writers spiritualize the images, leaving behind the more primitive ideas associated with religious sacrifice, such as the appeasement or paying off of an angry deity. But they do not expand or offer additional commentary on the metaphors, leaving the readers (the faith community) to make the connection between Jesus' death and the images.

In his letter to the Corinthians, Paul informs them that he "handed on" to them what he "had received" (as part of the common Christian tradition), namely, that "Christ died for our sins in accordance with the scriptures, and that he was buried, and that he was raised on the third day in accordance with the scriptures" (1 Cor 15:3–4). The background for this metaphor of Christ dying for our sins is found in the sacrifices for sins offered in the temple. According to temple theology during the time of Jesus, certain sins and impurities could only be remitted through sacrifice. The temple priests controlled this process and actually held an institutional monopoly on the forgiveness of sins. In other words, the temple system of sacrifice determined who had or did not have access to God.

When the early Christians said that Jesus died for our sins, or that he was the sacrifice for our sins, it had a subversive effect. They were pointing to Christ as the one who broke the temple monopoly on forgiveness. It was their way of saying that whatever might keep one from experiencing God's love, whatever might alienate one from God or from one's sisters and brothers in the human family, has been dealt with in Jesus. One does not need to go through the temple ritual of sacrifice. It was a statement of radical grace.

The English word "sacrifice" comes from a Latin word that means "to make sacred." In the Old Testament, most of the sacrifices involved offering a gift and sharing a meal.

The supreme gift is the offering of one's life to God. In writing to the Romans, Paul urged them to give their lives as a living sacrifice to God by not being conformed to the world, but by being transformed through the renewing of their minds (Rom 12:1–2).

Sacrifice is a word we use for those who give their lives for others. For example, late in the afternoon of Wednesday, January 13, 1982, Air Florida Flight 90 took off from Washington National Airport and plunged into the icy Potomac. Of the seventy-nine people on board, only six managed to escape onto the tail, which happened to stick up above the surface of the river. The rescue helicopter repeatedly dropped lines to them. Arland D. Williams Jr. repeatedly passed the lines to others and by the time five were saved, he had slipped under the water from hypothermia. In describing his death, it would be inadequate to simply say he drowned. The only proper headline would read, "Man Sacrifices His Life for Others." In this sense, his death was sacred.

This is what Jesus did. He gave his life for God's cause, for a vision of a world healed, made whole, and put to right. Nowhere in Luke's Gospel is Jesus' death portrayed as some sort of legal transaction like the paying of a debt or the remission of a penalty. Jesus died in pursuit of God's dream for the world, God's peaceable kingdom. His death marked the culmination of a life of humility, prophetic courage, compassion, nonviolence, and self-giving for the good of others.

Jesus died the way he lived. In Luke's Gospel, as Jesus is led away to Golgotha he identifies with those who will suffer in Jerusalem when the Romans lay siege to the city

(Luke 23:27–31). He offers grace to the criminals being crucified with him (Luke 23:39–43). He speaks a word of preemptive forgiveness toward his torturers and killers (Luke 23:34). Then finally, he commends his spirit to his Abba, his compassionate Father/Mother, the God whose kingdom he proclaimed and embodied. Never did he respond to violence with violence. On the night of his arrest, when one of his disciples drew his sword and cut off the ear of one of the servants of the high priest, Jesus responded by touching and healing him. He told his disciples to put up their swords (Luke 22: 49–51). He died the way he lived, revealing a God of nonviolence, grace, and forgiveness.

The atoning significance of Jesus' death in the Gospel of Luke is not substitution—Jesus is not dying in the place of anyone. Rather, the redeeming significance of Jesus' death in Luke is best described as participation. Earlier in the Gospel, on his journey to Jerusalem, Jesus tells his disciples that he will suffer, be rejected by the religious establishment, and be killed. Then he says, "If any want to become my followers, let them deny themselves and take up their cross daily and follow me" (Luke 9:23). He calls them to follow him on his way to the cross, to somehow participate with him in his death. He tells them that they must lose their lives in order to find their lives (Luke 9:24).

The living Christ calls us to deny ourselves, to relinquish our quest for revenge, to die to our desire to crush our opponents. We must not be burdened with bitterness or malice, or shackled by the need to respond to violence with violence. We are called to be Christ's emissaries of peace and agents of reconciliation. We are called to walk in the way of Jesus—the way of forgiveness and grace.

Jesus knew that the only way to break the escalating cycles of violence in the world, cycles into which most of us are drawn at some point in our lives, would be through nonviolence and forgiveness. Redemption and reconciliation are worked out in our lives, relationships, and communities as we participate with the living Christ in living, speaking, sharing, and exuding the way of forgiveness and nonviolence embodied in Jesus of Nazareth. At the end of Luke's Gospel, Jesus commissions his disciples to preach repentance/conversion and forgiveness of sins to all peoples (Luke 24:45–49). Conversion to the way of nonviolence, peace, and forgiveness is what the gospel of Jesus is all about.

As Jesus commends his spirit to the Father, he is not just thinking of his own future, he is thinking of the future of his disciples and the future of the world. When Jesus informs the disciples that he will die in Jerusalem, he also tells them that he will be raised. Jesus believed he would be vindicated. Jesus believed that the kingdom of God he proclaimed and embodied, God's new world of justice and peace, would prevail.

When Jesus sends his disciples out after his resurrection, he tells them that repentance and forgiveness of sins are to be proclaimed to "all nations, beginning from Jerusalem" (Luke 24:47). The good news of God's peaceable kingdom is for all people. In Luke's sequel, the book of Acts, Peter and John preach this good news in Jerusalem. They proclaim that Jesus, who was crucified by the powers that be, was raised, vindicated by the God of Israel. Peter then calls the people to decision. He says,

> Repent therefore, and turn to God so that your
> sins may be wiped out, so that times of refresh-
> ing may come from the presence of the Lord,
> and that he may send the Messiah appointed for
> you, that is, Jesus, who must remain in heaven
> until the time of universal restoration that God
> announced long ago through his holy prophets."
> Acts 3:19–21

God is going to set things right. The NRSV translates it as
"the time of universal restoration." Just as Jesus bore the evil
and hostility of the powers that be all the way to the cross,
so God will bear the sin of the world until such time when
all the world comes to repentance.

Universal restoration cannot come without repentance. The writer of 2 Peter puts it this way, "The Lord
. . . is patient with you, not wanting anyone to perish, but
everyone to come to repentance" (2 Pet 3:9). There is no
restoration, no regeneration, no healing, renewal, and reconciliation without repentance, without a change of mind,
heart, and direction. One must intentionally, Luke says
daily, take up the cross and follow the way of Jesus, the way
of nonviolence and forgiveness.

A good friend from a former pastorate sent me a paper that he had written for an online theology class. He had
wrongly assumed that one implication of universalism is
that there will be unrepentant persons in God's kingdom.
Every person I know who believes or hopes that eventually
all persons will be redeemed, contends that each individual
who enters God's kingdom enters through the process of repentance. No one experiences fullness of life in God's realm
without repentance.

Jesus emphasized the need for repentance. The Gospels summarize Jesus' message thus: "Repent, for the kingdom of God has come near" (see Mark 1:15). Jesus called people to change the way they think and to reorder their lives in alignment with the priorities and values of the kingdom of God.

This involves some remorse, regret, and sorrow for the hurt and harm we have caused others. Surely this means confronting and confessing our part and participation, both explicitly and implicitly, in acts and decisions that have diminished the lives of others.

A good illustration of the necessity of repentance can be found in chapter 5 of Paul's first letter to the Corinthians. It's hard to keep from smiling every time I read verse one—not from the meaning of the verse, but from a story I was told by a fellow seminary student years ago. We were working in a factory together and were on lunch break. I'm not sure how it got started, but three or four of us who were seminary students began talking about some of our mistakes and mishaps in ministry. Our friend told about the first funeral he conducted. He was nervous and very unsure of himself. At the graveside he planned to read 1 Corinthians 15, but had not marked the page. Instead of turning to 1 Corinthians 15, he turned to 1 Corinthians 5 and with great boldness (an attempt to compensate for his anxiety I suppose) he began reading, "It is actually reported that there is sexual immorality among you, and of a kind that is not found even among pagans; for a man is living with his father's wife." He was so nervous he did not even realize what he had read until he finished the verse. Once the toothpaste is out of the tube and on the brush, you might as well stick it in your mouth. I can't remember what my friend said to make things right.

Paul blasts the Corinthian church for not doing something about this. Paul says,

> And you are arrogant! Should you not rather have mourned, so that he who had done this would have been removed from among you? For though absent in body, I am present in spirit; and as if present I have already pronounced judgment in the name of the Lord Jesus on the man who has done such a thing. When you are assembled, and my spirit is present with the power of the Lord Jesus, you are to hand this man over to Satan for the destruction of the flesh, so that his spirit may be saved in the day of the Lord. 1 Cor 5:2–5

Paul tells them to render judgment (actually Paul is rendering judgment for them) by putting this man out of the fellowship, not in order to be condemned, but so that he will ultimately be restored and redeemed—that "his spirit may be saved in the day of the Lord." The purpose of the judgment is to bring about repentance.

I am hopeful that everyone will be redeemed. I can't say for certain that will happen, because we are all free creatures with the freedom to choose our own path. Many influences impact and limit our freedom, but no one enters the kingdom of God unless one chooses to. There may be persons so pervaded by evil, they never choose the ultimate good. I believe, however, that given enough consequences, enough "hells" to live through, and given enough opportunities, enough of God's wooing, drawing, luring, and persuading love, even the most resistant will one day come to repentance.

If the cross is a demonstration of God's patience, love, and endurance, then surely God will bear with sinners as long as it takes for sinners to see their sin and turn from their sinful ways. If we are lost, like the shepherd and the woman in the parables of Luke 15, God will seek us until God finds us. Of course, we have to want to be found, but God has all the time in the universe.

In the movie, *The Lord of the Rings: The Two Towers*, the screen version of the second volume of Tolkien's *Lord of the Rings* trilogy, Frodo and Sam find themselves lost in the Misty Mountains on their journey to Mount Doom to destroy the ring of power. Here they encounter Gollum, the previous possessor of the ring. Gollum is a dirty, ugly, pitiful creature, though very cunning. He is obsessed with regaining the ring. Gollum knows the way to Mount Doom and agrees to help them, secretly planning to steal the ring.

Sam is demeaning and degrading toward Gollum. Finally, Frodo confronts Sam.

"Why do you do that—call him names and run him down all the time?"

"Because that's what he is, Mr. Frodo. There's naught left in him but lies and deceit. It's the ring he wants. It's all he cares about."

Frodo knows the power of the ring. Looking sadly at Gollum, he says to Sam, "You have no idea what it did to him. I have to help him, Sam."

"Why?" asks Sam.

"Because I have to believe he can come back."

I love that last line. Why did Frodo have to believe? Because he knew the power of the ring. He knew its addictive, oppressive power. Do any of us know, for example, what a lifetime of abuse and oppression can do to someone? How that would limit one's capacity to respond to and choose the good? I agree with Frodo. *I believe that given different consequences and contexts, new influences and opportunities, and the luring, drawing, transforming influence of God's love, everyone will return to their true home and discover their true humanity.* I believe everyone will come to repentance.

Jesus bears the violence without reacting in violence. He absorbs it through forgiveness. He confidently commends his spirit to *Abba*, perhaps intuitively knowing that through his Spirit his followers will be able to bear it too. This is why we can call what happened on Friday of Holy Week "good."

Jesus set in motion a movement, a movement that the living Christ continues today in collaboration, cooperation, and communion with all who act justly, pursue mercy, and walk humbly with God, each another, and all creation. It is a movement of nonviolence and peacemaking, of forgiveness and reconciliation. A movement to which we are called—in the words of Paul or one of his disciples—to "be imitators of God, as beloved children, and live in love, as Christ loved us and gave himself up for us, a fragrant offering and sacrifice to God" (Eph 5:1–2).

Forgive us, O God, for turning the cross into a symbol of organized religion. For making the cross some sort of legal transaction that gives us a ticket to heaven, without our having to

*daily take up our cross and follow the way of Jesus. Save us
from our Americanized, consumerist versions of Christianity
and turn us into real followers of the Christ, committed to
nonviolence, forgiveness, sacrifice, and peacemaking, no
matter what the cost. Most of us, Lord, have about enough
Christianity to make us immune to the real thing. Shake us
up and turn us loose to infect the world with the real disease,
which is the cure for the evil that lurks in every human heart.
In the name of the one who is the true prince of peace we pray.
Amen.*

In the face of active or direct evil or violence, the refusal
to respond in kind is a powerful, chosen act, not a mere
passive submission. Refusing to return evil for evil unmasks
the violence of the evil acts, and demonstrates that the evil
which killed Jesus originated with humankind and not with
God. . . . Jesus' mission was to make present and visible the
reign of God. That mission meant witnessing to and pre-
senting God's unmerited forgiveness and reconciliation of
sinners to God.[1]

Jesus died to maintain the integrity of his life. Or, to reverse
Mel Gibson's claim in *The Passion of the Christ*, "Living Was
His Reason for Dying." His nonviolent resistance to violence
as a revelation of God's own character was consummated
by that execution. We have no word for the crucifixion of
Christ other than "sacrifice," a making sacred of both life
and death, a gift both to divinity and to humanity.[2]

---

1. Weaver, *The Nonviolent Atonement*, 40–41.
2. Crossan, *The Greatest Prayer*, 111.

What immediately follows from the scapegoat story of Leviticus 16 is what is called "The Law of Holiness" (Leviticus 17–27), which largely defines holiness as *separation from evil*—which is exactly what they had just ritualized. Three thousand years later human consciousness hasn't moved a great deal beyond that, despite the message of the cross. *Jesus does not define holiness as separation from evil as much as absorption and transformation of it, wherein I pay the price instead of always asking others to pay the price.* It moves from the persistent myth of redemptive violence to the divine plan of redemptive suffering. I would say only a small minority of Christianity ever got the point. Maybe because when it asked us to do the same, we backed away from it as a life agenda and made it into a cosmic transaction between Jesus and the Father. Traditional atonement theories asked a lot of Jesus but little of us, except lots of thank-yous.[3]

3. Rohr, *Things Hidden*, 143.

8

Choosing Life

Early on the first day of the week, while it was still dark, Mary Magdalene came to the tomb and saw that the stone had been removed from the tomb. So she ran and went to Simon Peter and the other disciple, the one whom Jesus loved, and said to them, "They have taken the Lord out of the tomb, and we do not know where they have laid him." Then Peter and the other disciple set out and went toward the tomb. The two were running together, but the other disciple outran Peter and reached the tomb first. He bent down to look in and saw the linen wrappings lying there, but he did not go in. Then Simon Peter came, following him, and went into the tomb. He saw the linen wrappings lying there, and the cloth that had been on Jesus' head, not lying with the linen wrappings but rolled up in a place by itself. Then the other disciple, who reached the tomb first, also went in, and he saw and believed; for as yet they did not understand the scripture, that he must rise from the dead. Then the disciples returned to their homes.

But Mary stood weeping outside the tomb. As she wept, she bent over to look into the tomb; and she saw two angels in white, sitting where the body of Jesus had been lying, one at the head and the other at the feet. They said to her, "Woman, why are you weeping?" She said to them, "They have taken away my Lord, and I do not know where they have laid him." When she had said this, she turned around and saw Jesus standing there, but she did not know that it was Jesus. Jesus said to her, "Woman, why are you weeping? Whom are you looking for?" Supposing him to be the gardener, she said to him, "Sir, if you have carried him away, tell me where you have laid him, and I will take him away." Jesus said to her, "Mary!" She turned and said to him in Hebrew, "Rabbouni!" (which means Teacher). Jesus said to her, "Do not hold on to me, because I have not yet ascended to the Father. But go to my brothers and say to them, 'I am ascending to my Father and your Father, to my God and your God.'" Mary Magdalene went and announced to the disciples, "I have seen the Lord"; and she told them that he had said these things to her. John 20:1–18.

IN FLANNERY O'Connor's story, *A Good Man is Hard to Find*, the Misfit is a notorious outlaw who has terrorized and murdered a family after they had an automobile accident on an isolated rural road. He is now holding the grandmother hostage. She is overwhelmed with grief and stricken with fear. She cries out, "Jesus . . . Jesus!" And in response the Misfit says, "Jesus was the only One who ever raised the dead, and He shouldn't have done it. He's thrown everything off balance. If He did what He said, then it's nothing for you to do but throw everything away and follow Him, and if He didn't, then it's nothing for you to do but enjoy the few minutes you got left the best way you can—by killing somebody or burning down his house or doing some other meanness to him."[1]

Even the Misfit recognizes that if Jesus really is the real thing, then "he's thrown everything off balance." Through Jesus life breaks forth into the realm of death and throws everything off balance.

Death and life are poignant, theologically packed symbols in John's Gospel. Death is not so much the grim reaper who visits each one of us at the end of our days on earth, as it is a state or realm in which many of us currently dwell. In John, *death is primarily a living death.*

We all know, I think, what it is like to live in the realm of death. It can take the form of a deep, dark depression, an enslaving addiction, an abusive relationship, or any oppressive situation. To be possessed by our possessions, to be controlled by greed, to be consumed with envy or malice, or to be numb with boredom is to live in a state of death.

Mary Magdalene is in a place of death. She is distraught, confused, bewildered, and angry. What else is there to do but cry? The one in whom she had placed her hope for a better tomorrow is gone. Not even his body remains. He had treated her with compassion and respect; he had entrusted her with responsibility and called her to follow him, even though it was unheard of for a rabbi to treat women with such dignity in that patriarchal world. Jesus did, and she was his disciple.

1. O'Connor, *The Complete Stories*, 132.

She believed he was the Messiah. The religious leaders, however, flatly rejected his message and ministry. He was brought before Pilate and sentenced to die. And die he did. She was there—watching. John says she was "near the cross," along with Jesus' mother and some other women (19:25). She witnessed his agony, the cruelty, the degradation and humiliation. She felt his pain and sorrow. She was there when he took his last breath, just after he cried, "It is finished."

Now, she thought, they have taken away his body. Maybe she had come to say a final goodbye, to have closure. A cloud of despair is hovering over her. She is in a place of death.

But then, suddenly, breaking into the stillness—a voice. A startling intrusion into the world of death. It is Jesus speaking her name, but she does not recognize him. This is a recurring feature in the appearance stories. Jesus is not immediately recognized.

There may have been something very different about his appearance, but I suspect that the Gospel writers were mostly making a theological point. Jesus can no longer be with his disciples in the same way he was prior to his death. No longer can he be a physical, tangible, and visible presence. Perhaps this is the significance of his words to Mary, "Do not hold on to me, for I have not yet returned to the Father." He cannot be with her and the others as he was before.

Jesus had tried to prepare them. Jesus told them that he was going to the Father, but he would not leave them as orphans, he would come to them. He promised them that he and the Father would send "another *Paraclete*" (the

Greek word), variously translated as Counselor, Comforter, or Advocate—one like Jesus, the Spirit of Truth. The Spirit, says Jesus in the Gospel of John, "abides with you, and shall be in you" (John 14:17). This is Jesus' way of saying that the Spirit would take his place, that the Spirit would mediate, illuminate, and reveal the grace, truth, and reality of Christ.

In John 14, as Jesus prepares the disciples for his departure, he says, "In a little while the world will no longer see me, but you will see me; because I live, you also will live" (14:19). Seeing and living go hand in hand. All this mystical language is hard to nail down, but what Jesus seems to be telling them is that after he departs, he will come to them, but not as he was before, not as a physical or tangible presence. Rather, he will be a spiritual presence. *In his earthly ministry he was with them as a physical presence, but in his resurrected state he would be in them as a spiritual presence.*

All of us, like Mary, have trouble recognizing Jesus. When the mind is befuddled and perplexed, when the heart is fearful, fretful, and weighed down by loss and grief, when the spirit is crushed and broken, it's difficult to recognize Christ. When Jesus speaks Mary's name, suddenly she sees and knows that it is Jesus. While such recognition often comes to us by way of the gathered Christian community, the experience is very personal.

Seminary professor Tom Long tells about the time when, as a seminary student, he served an internship at a church where he provided pastoral care to families. One of the families under his charge was quite large, and their youngest child, Robert, had cerebral palsy. More often than not, when he visited the family they would be gathered together in a large group, at the dinner table or in the den, laughing and telling stories, but not Robert. Robert always seemed to be on the outside of those gatherings, watching the others.

On one occasion, it was just Dr. Long and the mother visiting together. After some small talk, she told him about something that had happened just a few days before. She was sitting in the family room in the late afternoon, and Robert was standing in the darkness down the hall, watching from a distance. She felt what she described as a "strange shift in the room." She looked up from her knitting, down the hallway toward Robert. She told Dr. Long that she saw Jesus with his arm around Robert's shoulder. She looked away, looked again, and there was only Robert. But she was convinced that she saw Jesus.

Dr. Long says that to this day he's not sure what to make of it. At the time, he decided to psychoanalyze the event, thinking that she probably felt so guilty about the ways they had excluded Robert that she was projecting her failings through the symbol system of the Christian faith. And yet, the mother was convinced that she saw Jesus, and did anyone really have the authority or the knowledge to tell her it was just a projection? After that experience, the mother was not the same. It was a personal experience, but it didn't remain personal. She went to work in the community and started several programs for children with disabilities.[2] When Christ speaks to us and makes his will known (and he can do that in all sorts of ways), it is often for the purpose of advancing the well-being of the larger community. The living Christ seeks friends, partners, and coworkers to participate with him in God's

2. Referenced by Ramsey, "Conversion," 33.

kingdom on earth. If this mother had listened to someone telling her that the whole thing was a projection due to her repressed guilt, maybe she would have not changed. Who knows? She believed, however, that she saw Jesus, and her life changed course.

One thing that often happens when we begin to "see" and "hear" Jesus is a shift in the way we see and hear others and the way we evaluate our place in the world. As the Misfit says, Jesus throws everything off balance. Our world is altered. *When Jesus takes center stage we experience a repositioning of our ultimate reference point. No longer is it just about "me" and my story or even "us" and our particular group's story. Jesus draws us into a larger story that is much more inclusive—the kingdom of God.*

In John's Gospel, this is described as a movement (a crossing over) from the state of death into the realm of life (5:24). When Mary hears Jesus speak her name a seismic shift occurs in her world. Everything is thrown off balance. The irony for all of us is that this shaking of our life's hopes and dreams leads to the construction of a new foundation for life that is indestructible.

Unless one has undergone this sort of conversion, it is not likely that one will grasp what Jesus meant when he said, "Seek first the kingdom of God." The world doesn't understand how on Easter Sunday destitute and impoverished Haitians who have lost loved ones and who own nothing, can gather in the streets in Port-au-Prince after the devastating earthquake, dancing and singing. Anderson Cooper of CNN looked on and remarked, "Don't they know what others are saying about how bad it really is?"

Oh, they know. They feel the impact and see the horrific effects of the tragedy everyday. They know that they are living in the midst of death, but they also have decided not to be overcome by death. They have determined not to live in the realm of death, even though death is all about them.

Many of us live in the midst of death and don't even know it. In our consumerist, self-indulgent, wasteful culture, death is all about us, too—in the form of emptiness, greed, boredom, addiction, prejudice, and arrogance. But if we choose to let it, life has a way of breaking through the dark clouds, shining into our hearts.

Our circumstances may not change at all. Our situation may remain the same. The problems may continue to pile up. But we are different. There is a shift in our thinking. We see with new eyes and hear with new ears. We are compelled to participate in God's movement to heal, renew, and restore lives, communities, and the good earth we inhabit. We are inspired to work for and invest in the good of others, to spread a vision of life—of relationships reconciled, of resources more equitably distributed, of wrongs made right.

It may be something as simple as writing a note of apology, asking forgiveness for a wrong done, sending a letter of encouragement, volunteering in the soup kitchen, or visiting in the nursing home. Or it may be something as large as putting pressure on our representatives for the promotion of policies and laws that help our environment and provide for more equitable distribution of resources. It may be something as challenging as protesting for nuclear disarmament. (In the prophets, it was beating swords into plowshares; in our case, it is disassembling nuclear bombs and using the parts for scrape metal.) Or it may be something as simple as keeping a stretch of road clean and free of trash.

Life has broken into our world, and Life is calling our names, but we have to decide, we have to choose. *In the Gospel of John, belief has less to do with what we actually believe about Jesus and more to do with being faithful to the way of Jesus.* The decision of faith is a decision regarding how we will live. Will we allow the malevolent, malignant powers of death to diminish and denigrate our lives, or will we choose to live in the hope, vitality, and abundance of resurrection life?

I heard about a man named Ed, who divorced in midlife and moved back in with his elderly parents. Gradually, he took over their care. Almost weekly he would visit the pastor in his office and complain about what a burden his parents were to him, and how they kept him from being able to date or do anything worthwhile. He complained about how they took up all his time and money, and what a drain they were. His weekly visits wore the pastor down.

After several years, his parents both died within a six-month period. The pastor thought, "Now Ed will finally be happy and he won't come in with all his complaints." And sure enough, that was the case for about three weeks. Then Ed turned up again at the Pastor's door. "I miss them so much," he sighed. "They were the best parents anyone could wish for. My life is so empty without them."

Most pastors would just accept their fate. But this pastor decided to be a real friend and spiritual guide to Ed. He said, "Ed, your life is not empty. Your glass is full of all your favorite things: discontent, misery, an 'if only' attitude, a 'things will be great when' mind-set. You are a person who enjoys being unhappy. Face it and embrace it. It is your identity. It is who you are."[3]

You see what this courageous pastor was trying to do, don't you? He was trying to shake Ed up, bring about some kind of shift in his world, throw him off balance, so that he might choose life instead of death.

Seminary professor Alyce McKenzie shares about the time when she was a pastor and received a call from a parishioner around ten o'clock in the evening. The voice on the other end of the phone said, "My nephew is very distraught. He's even willing to talk to a minister. Can you meet with him?" She said she would.

Twenty minutes later she was sitting in her living room across from a young man in his twenties. He was pale as a paper towel and on his temple was a deep gash that had just been stitched. He and his friend had been to a local bar and had a few drinks. He was driving them home and ran off the road. All he had were four stitches in his head, but his friend was fighting for his life in ICU.

On the coffee table in front of where the young man sat was one of those big Bibles with the head of Christ on the front cover. As he told his story, he ran his fingertips over the face of Jesus, tracing the outline over and over again. When he finished, he looked up at Rev. McKenzie and said, "Jesus Christ, what am I going to do?" It was a cry of desperation. More of a curse than a prayer.

She told him that he had two options. He could begin his sentence of suffering by drowning his pain with alcohol and destroying his spirit with guilt. Or he could turn his

3. McKenzie, "Do You Want to Be Made Well?" 135.

curse into a prayer and really ask, "Jesus Christ, what am I going to do?"[4]

We, too, have a choice. The Gospel of John offers it up to us in many rich and colorful ways. We can decide to eat from the bread of life and drink from the spring of living water. We can decide, like the invalid in John 5, that we really want to be made whole, and we can hear Jesus say, "Take up your mat and walk." We can decide to follow the Good Shepherd who lays down his life for the sheep. We can, like Lazarus in the tomb, hear Jesus say, "Come forth." And with Mary Magdalene, we can hear Jesus call out our names and say to us, as he later says to Mary and the other disciples, "As the Father sent me, so I send you." We have a choice.

We can choose to be bitter and hate those we feel have done us wrong. We can choose to grasp, grab, and cling to whatever we think will give us some leverage over others. We can choose to pursue our selfish ambitions and climb the ladder of success without any regard for those we have to step over or step on to move up. We can choose to drown in self-pity, bemoaning our bad luck and suffering. We can choose death. Or we can choose to relinquish our pride, greed, and egotism. We can choose to forgive and pray for healing for ourselves and those we have hurt or who have hurt us. We can decide to forget about our own agenda of upward mobility, and reach out to those who have been marginalized and forgotten. We can choose to make the best we can of a terrible situation. We can choose to transform our pain, rather than transmit it to others. We can choose life.

4. Ibid., 137–38.

What will it be? Choose Life.

Gracious Lord, give us ears to hear the living Christ calling our names, calling us to embrace a higher purpose, calling us to participate in a larger story—your story of redemption and grace. Give us, today, the courage, the inner fortitude and faith to say "no" to death and "yes" to Life. In Jesus' name, Amen.

Christ's death and his resurrection are the two sides of the one single happening which is often termed 'the Christ event.' . . . The cross and the resurrection stand in the same relation to one another as death and eternal life. Since death makes every life historical, death has to be seen as the power of history. Since resurrection brings the dead into eternal life and means the annihilation of death, it breaks the power of history and is itself the end of history. If we keep the two together, then the cross of Christ comes to stand at the apocalyptic end of world history, and the raising of the dead at the beginning of the new creation of the world.[5]

The early Christian faith in the resurrection was not based solely on Christ's appearances. It was just as strongly motivated, at the very least, by the experience of God's Spirit. Paul therefore calls this Spirit 'the Spirit' or 'power' of the resurrection. Luke makes the end of the appearances with Christ's ascension be followed by the outpouring of the pentecostal Spirit. Believing in the risen Christ means being possessed by the Spirit of the resurrection. In the Spirit, the presence of the living Christ was experienced. Believing in Christ's resurrection therefore does not mean affirming a

5. Moltmann, *The Way of Jesus Christ*, 214.

fact. It means being possessed by the life-giving Spirit and participating in the powers of the age to come (Heb. 6.5).[6]

Resurrection is not a deferred consolation—'the opium of the next world.' It is the power which enables this life to be reborn. The hope is directed, not towards a different world but towards the redemption of this one. In the Spirit, resurrection is not merely expected; it is already experienced. Resurrection happens every day. In love we experience many deaths and many resurrections. We experience resurrection by being born again to a living hope through love, in which we already, here and now, wake from death to life, and through liberation: 'Where the Spirit of the Lord is, there is freedom' (II Cor. 3.17).[7]

6. Ibid., 218.
7. Ibid., 242.

Bibliography

Berry, Wendell. *Jayber Crow*. Berkeley, CA: Counterpoint, 2000.

Cortright, David. "Finding the Way Out." *Sojourners* 40 (March 2011) 14–17.

Crossan, John Dominic. *The Greatest Prayer: Rediscovering the Revolutionary Message of the Lord's Prayer*. New York: HarperOne, 2010.

Hall, John Douglas. *The Cross in Our Context: Jesus and the Suffering World*. Minneapolis: Fortress, 2003.

Jones, L. Gregory. *Embodying Forgiveness: A Theological Analysis*. Grand Rapids: Eerdmans, 1995.

Manning, Brennan. *Ruthless Trust: The Ragamuffin's Path to God*. San Francisco: HarperCollins, 2000.

McKenzie, Alyce M. "Do You Want to Be Made Well?" In *Preaching John's Gospel: The World It Imagines*, edited by David Fleer and David Bland, 134–38. St Louis: Chalice, 2008.

Miller, Arthur. *The Death of a Salesman*. New York: Viking, 1949.

Moltmann, Jurgen. "Prisoner of Hope." In *Bread and Wine: Readings for Lent and Easter*, 146–52. Farmington, PA: The Plough Publishing House, 2003.

———. *The Way of Jesus Christ: Christology in Messianic Dimensions*. Translated by Margaret Kohl. Minneapolis: Fortress, 1993.

Nouwen, Henri. *Making All Things New: An Invitation to the Spiritual Life*. New York: HarperSanFrancisco, 1981.

———. *The Essential Henri Nouwen*. Edited by Robert A. Jonas. Boston: Shambhala, 2009.

O'Connor, Flannery. *The Complete Stories*. New York: Farrar, Straus and Giroux, 1971.

Ramsey, Mark. "Conversion." *JP* 34 (Easter, 2011) 33–37.

Rohr, Richard. *Falling Upward: A Spirituality for the Two Halves of Life.* San Francisco: Jossey-Bass, 2011.

———. *Things Hidden: Scripture as Spirituality.* Cincinnati: St Anthony Messenger, 2008.

Soelle, Dorothee, "On This Gallows." In *Bread and Wine: Readings for Lent and Easter*, 175–78. Farmington, PA: The Plough Publishing House, 2003.

Steindl-Rast, David. *Deeper Than Words: Living the Apostle's Creed.* New York: Doubleday/Image, 2010.

Stoner, Eric. "The Human Toll." *Sojourners* 40 (March 2011) 18–21.

Vanier, Jean. *Becoming Human.* New York: Paulist, 1998.

———. *Community and Growth*, Revised ed. New York: Paulist, 1989.

Weaver, J. Denny. *The Nonviolent Atonement.* Grand Rapids: Eerdmans, 2001.

Willard, Dallas. *The Divine Conspiracy: Rediscovering Our Hidden Life in God.* San Francisco: HarperCollins, 1998.

Willimon, William H. With a foreword by Marva J. Dawn. *Thank God It's Friday: Encountering the Seven Last Words from the Cross.* Nashville: Abingdon, 2006.

Yancey, Philip. *The Jesus I Never Knew.* Grand Rapids: Zondervan, 1995.

www.ingramcontent.com/pod-product-compliance
Lightning Source LLC
Chambersburg PA
CBHW071059090426
42737CB00013B/2394